Sleep Is No Comfort
Essays

By
Kevin Minh Allen

Published by,
CQT Media And Publishing

ISBN-13: 9780988585881

© 2019 CQT Media And Publishing. An Archival micro imprint.

*Publisher's note: The formatting of this book is intentional,
mirroring the spaces and systems to which it belongs.*

Table of Contents

RE-IMMERSE

NO DREAM TOO LASTING

QUALMS

5

RE-IMMERSE

Communal Haircuts

For much of my life my hair styles have been all over the place, from bad to worse, from passable to entirely fitting. My parents favored the typical comb-down, no-frills "bowl cut" when I was a wee one, and I have to say that I was a rather cute tyke despite it. As a self-conscious, but needing-to-be-cool-at-all-costs teenager I wanted the "feathered" look that Ponch wore on the TV show CHiPs, so my mom took me to her hairdresser to get it done. The end result looked like a wilting hair helmet. In my rebellious metalhead phase between junior high and sophomore year of high school I let the hair on the back of my head grow past my shoulders (and let my budding facial hair grow into gnarly patches). Once I outgrew these adventures in childhood coif-dom, I simply settled on a shaved head and discovered the wonderful symmetrical dome shape of my skull. I didn't have to comb my hair and I saved a ton on shampoo. It wasn't until I lived in Seattle when I found what my hair was truly missing all these years: the Vietnamese touch!

For the majority of the years I lived in Seattle, I went to a small Vietnamese hair salon in the Little Saigon district called Lyn Hair Salon. I can't remember how I found it, whether someone recommended it to me or by driving around and coincidentally seeing it. What secured my affinity for it was that it represented one of many steps I took toward linking myself to my Vietnamese heritage. I listened intently sometimes to the conversations in Vietnamese between patrons and hairdressers and the breezy way they laughed. I gauged whether they were sharing a good story, having a disagreement or asking questions. The salon served as one of the few linguistic oases where native speakers could congregate and be accepted and completely understood. I met "Lyn" early on and I remember her being kind, attentive and very capable. We made small talk and like most Vietnamese who encounter a mixed-race person she asked me if I was Vietnamese. I'm generally wary of small talk, but I made a slight exception for this woman, so I told her that I was part Vietnamese and that I had been born in Saigon during the war and I don't know who my parents are. Instead of the usual recriminations I receive from Vietnamese people after I tell them of the unknown particulars of my life — how I should know/learn Vietnamese, that I'm much better off here than in Vietnam, etc. — Lyn smiled, acknowledged what I said and proceeded to ask me how I would like my hair cut. That was the first indication I would be a regular at this hair salon.

On the photo sharing website Flickr I follow a couple of accounts that post old scanned and archived photos from Vietnam throughout the past century-and-a-half. The majority of them feature images of French colonial life and its trappings during the occupation. Hidden within these collections are a few photos showing men getting haircuts on city streets. My interest in looking at photos taken of an otherwise banal activity may appear odd, but I admittedly fixate on odd minutiae that make me think of life at odd angles. Few of the photos taken of daily life in Vietnam during those eras appear to cover what people did when not fearing for their lives or burying their dead. When faced with the knowledge that your routine could be upended at any moment, your body savaged or life taken in an instant, keeping up appearances would help keep you sane. The image of a man getting a haircut speaks to his desire to maintain proper hygiene and keep up with current fashion. Looking at black-and-white photos of men getting haircuts decades ago provide me an open time capsule buried in a land in which I would arrive at the end of 1973. It makes me wonder how often men of means had their hair cut, whether the preferred coiffure changed with each incoming and outgoing superpower, how much a barber charged for a haircut, how long a haircut would take and how much mousse would be used considering the climate in Vietnam. Barbers and hairdressers must have had to contend with a whole set of different environmental factors that would affect the texture and volume of their customer's hair, not to mention how these men washed and maintained their dos.

Now, 40 years after two or three generations of Vietnamese refugees and immigrants have settled all over the world, hairstyles have evolved to adhere to the finicky tastes of fashion. But the root (pardon the pun) knowledge and understanding of what kind of haircut goes with a Vietnamese face lies in the familiar and caring hands of the hairdresser. In the hands of Lyn and later on another hairdresser, who became the main employee at the salon, I could sit back in the chair and let their expertise and intuition lead them to sculpt my hair. The fact that the hairdresser was of the same ethnicity as me gave me a sense of pride and confidence in my overall appearance. After I would pay and bid adieu to the ladies until next time, it never failed that my consciousness took a step back and reminded itself that it took so long to start to feel at ease within my mixed-race Vietnamese male skin, the one that I wished so badly I could peel off and throw back onto the streets of Saigon. In spite of the hairdressers at Lyn Hair Salon intuitively knowing which hairstyle fit my Asian features the best, the ever-present "imposter syndrome," which many adopted persons internalize, crept in and stirred debate about whether or not I should return.

My hair has been with (and on) me for all of my life, but I barely have gotten used to it and I still show it no remorse. Back when I was 20, I had impetuously shaved off all my hair for the very first time. The motive behind it was because I was studying abroad in Vienna, Austria and I needed to shed the old to bring in the new. My brown-skinned body was residing in a majority white foreign country and knew it had been an outcast within a majority white locale for most of its life because of its perceived foreignness. Absorbing the day-to-day student existence in Vienna began making me feel I was living someone else's life, so I wanted to do something symbolic — in a quite dramatic way — to honor that feeling of döppelgangerism. Without much hesitation, I picked up a pair of scissors and chopped off my wavy black locks. I then stepped into the shower, sprayed a mound of shaving cream in each palm, spread it onto my scalp and slowly, and a bit arduously, swiped a twin razor blade from front to back, over and over, moving in tight rows, until all the tufts of hair were removed, and my pale scalp slowly revealed itself.

I still have the photo of the final result. My profile is fuzzy, but it shows a couple dabs of shaving cream still clinging to my head. I have quite a satisfied look on my face because I finally felt liberated from the memory of my parents treating my full head of hair as if it were their own personal pea patch. Both of them wanted my hair shorn, trimmed, chopped and teased all in the name of trying to make it "look halfway decent" for whatever company we were about to receive at whichever upcoming function. My childhood head of hair was thick and exhibited an obstinate cowlick that sprouted a prominent ducktail. My parents must have been perplexed as to the hybrid consistency of my hair's Asian black tint and weaving, wavy curls. These traits betrayed both the Vietnamese and the American in me: Impossible to keep straight and futile to completely bring under control.

Currently, I no longer live in the city where Lyn Hair Salon is, and I have not yet taken the time to look for another hair salon/barber that serves a predominately Asian clientele where I live now. Well, let's rewind a bit here because I just remembered a really good illustration of how important it is for me to retain the services of an ethnically-appropriate hair dresser. Prior to moving back to my hometown, I decided to get an inexpensive haircut at one of those mall-friendly hair-cutleries. A young white woman signed me in and had me plop down in one of those plastic plushy chairs. She seemed to be in a bit of hurry and a little too chatty for my tastes. As soon as she grabbed for the electric clippers and started in on her version of a "fade," after I briefly instructed her on the cut I wanted, she was racing around my head and making boring small talk. A couple of times she lightly grazed the top of my ear with the clippers which made me increasingly nervous. The haircut took no more than six or seven minutes. If you're in a time crunch and will readily accept just anything, then I guess a speedy haircut would be a bonus. However, I expected attention to detail and a sharp professional touch. Unfortunately, I took it for granted that the hairdresser followed my instructions to the T and would make my do look like what I had taken for granted at Lyn's. No. The fade was un-even and it consequently made my head appear a bit lopsided. Suffice it to say, I've decided to let my hair grow until I can find a proper hairdresser who knows biracial Asian hair. In the meantime, if my silvery locks reach the length when they start to curl into my ear hole, then I'll plop down a few bucks just to get my head shaved.

I Am Nothing (and That is Something)

It was December 2013, and I was reaching my 40th year of life on this planet. On my way to Reno, Nevada, driving on Route 395, and nearing Susanville, California, I veered off the highway and onto its wide shoulder and then came to a stop. Dusk was settling in, darkness prevailed and no other cars were on the long, winding road except mine. The moon was a thin, shining crescent sitting in a black void. The pitch dark land stretched for miles on end in every direction and nothing seemed to be stirring out in that featureless expanse. I felt this overwhelming urge to get my backpack out of the trunk and just walk until I couldn't see the car anymore. Such soothing emptiness and silence beckoned me like the promise of a fearless Oblivion where my mind could forever rest. I sought solace and relief from ever-changing circumstances to have a better understanding how far I had come.

I had been born either face-up or face-down, either screaming until I was red in the face or holding in all my breath until my body turned blue. Either my mother was given the chance to hold me within the first few minutes of my birth and look upon my face or I was given over to someone else's outstretched arms and placed in a room crammed with other bawling newborns to stare at an oscillating ceiling fan blurring the senses. Either my father was there in the room to count my toes and fingers or he was a ghost just like my mother. I couldn't tell you because I just don't know. Perhaps I would know the whole story if someone who witnessed my entrance into the world could get word to me. But, I've been told before that that is asking for far too much.

There are no quick-and-easy answers as to why I chose to celebrate such a momentous stage in my life by myself. All I know is that I just wanted to drive very far away from the familiar. I wanted no friends and no family around me to celebrate the supposed day of my birth; wanted no one at all to revel in my slow accumulation of years in this space I temporarily occupy. In order to properly commemorate that significant year of birth, I needed to be alone.

I live with no illusions regarding my beginnings. Most likely, my parents are dead. That is the Unknown I believe in because I fear that the Truth will never ring true to me. Mind you, I don't mean that they are dead to me. In the moving pictures of my mind I imagine them talking. Without any sort of mementos or photographs to go on, I pretend their conversations revolve around re-living the moment when they wished they had, or had not, met in Vietnam, kissed in Vietnam, made love in Vietnam, and met their demise in Vietnam. My memories of my parents are fantasies, little tall tales I tell myself every time my reflection sees itself on the other side of the mirror. I have no trouble recognizing myself, but I probably would never recognize either one of my parents, even if they passed by me on the same side of the street. I disappeared into another land, another language, another family. Thigh-high snow drifts in the winter and rollicking pool parties in the summer are what I grew up with—not wilting palm trees and morning alms for shuffling monks outside the temple.

In a decades-old essay, I ended it by writing, "I slipped into this world, and I will slip out of it." It's a clever thought, albeit a nihilistic one. This feeling rises in me whenever life lets me down, but I eventually balance things out by realizing that there doesn't have to be a grand, relatable reason for me to live my life as I see fit. I don't overwhelm myself with thoughts of searching for any real reason for me to exist in this particular place at this exact moment in time. The road trip to celebrate my birthday was a momentous journey that brought me back to myself. I won't contend that I felt centered; just that I knew I was all right with the world and that my presence, no matter how long it lasted, was worthwhile.

My father and my mother may be gone, but I'm still here, their son. Yes, I am still nothing. I am nothing but a man who drives fourteen hours to a city

in the dead of winter where no one knows him and no
one ever will.

Fathered

The proverbial elephant sitting in my life's room
has been my circumstantial birth to an American man
and a Vietnamese woman during one of America's
most morally ambiguous wars. The mere thought of
such racial inter-mixing sets off strong reactions in
certain people and produces many loaded
assumptions about the parental lineage of the
offspring and the very worth of the offspring
themselves. Newspaper articles, books and TV shows
have examined the Amerasian angle for all it's worth,
but they invariably come away with a dramatic re-
creation that skims over a traumatic irreconcilable
existence that has harmed the person in question,
every time he attempts to live as an individual whose
past is irreducible.

As a product of the late '80s and early '90s, I was
not spared the national political rhetoric around war
and remembrance. This caught me off guard and left
me no alternative but to fall for the clichéd romance
of the farmer-turned-soldier surviving nightly
ambushes in the jungle and finding comfort in the
arms of a pretty native woman who sang him to sleep
while fanning his red, sweaty face with her rice hat.
Ill-trained in peeling back nuance and looking past
the simplistic melodrama, my imagination was
coaxed into labeling my biological father the enemy
of my enemy. I demonized the man because he wasn't
here to defend himself and no one presented any

evidence to contradict my assumptions. His absence made it easy for me to dress him up in fatigues and stab him repeatedly, jerking his body back and forth on my blade of contempt. With no on holding me back, I held the world up for ransom and demanded answers. My blinding anger pushed me onwards.

What made me sick to my stomach sometimes was the slow realization that my unknown father's DNA was an integral part of the construction of my physical body. During a lull in the day, I'd catch myself glaring in the mirror deciding which parts of me I wanted to cut off in order to feel complete again. Yet, there were other times when he appeared in my dreams as a doting father bending over his young protégé, smiling, ready to lift him up onto his shoulders. There were times I'd pretend to tell him about a new hobby, or what sport I was trying out for, or what mattered the most to me at the moment. In spite of it all, I continued living on without him, finding it difficult to readily trust in anyone because of this strange absence hanging around me.

The curtain of normalcy in my adoptive family decorated much of my childhood and adolescence until the glaring discrepancies that jarred loose the facts of my life. The erosion of any emotional attachment to my adoptive father as my eyes grew wider had a deep effect on how I viewed his role in my life. I suspected he noticed the same this separation occurring and it may have affected how he chose to treat me in his remaining years. Out of a healthy dose of fear and a dash of respect, I hid from my adoptive father how much I wanted to be like all the other little boys whose fathers physically resembled them. I was acutely aware of my illegitimacy among other boys when I was in the company of my adoptive father, especially when they began to look from me to him and from him to me. Instead of standing there like a paper son anymore, I started seeing my adoptive father as a surrogate with whom I wanted to replace with the man who sired me. It was up to me to erase the doubt in the other kids' minds as to whether or not I belonged to a family of my own.

There were many days and nights when I thought the only real emotion I possessed was anger. Although I was good at throwing it under the bed and hiding it, the unresolved anger would inevitably transform into an inhuman beast that jumped out of nowhere and at the most inconvenient of times. Plus, the one whom I called "Dad" my whole life passed down his own short fuse for me to add to my simmering fuse box. I constantly lived with the feeling that there were swaths of uncontrollable wildfires eating their way through my rugged subconscious. One can only imagine what kind of rueful young man I had become. Some of those infernos I attributed to the man who, for reasons only known to him, failed to come and claim me as his flesh and blood when I was born.

My adoptive family simply became collateral damage when they found themselves directly on the war path aimed at my biological father. In my own immature way I had cut a deal between my pride and my insecurity to convince myself that if my own father didn't want me, then to hell with anyone who dared lay claim over me. This arrangement explains why I felt so ostracized from the family unit. But looking back on it now, I admit to actually doing most of the pushing out of myself from their care and attention. By rejecting their sphere of influence, I held deeply to the belief that the man who made up the other half of my DNA had decided to cut himself out my life.

Well-meaning people still try to convince me that my biological parents made the right decision to sacrifice their own happiness, and possibly their own lives, so that I may be given the chance to live a life in relative safety. I always knew they were simply poo-pooing any sense of hurt I gave off during those rare, naïve moments when I would tell others my origin story. Watching them cry their crocodile tears, I usually imagine wrapping that obligatory gratitude they need me to demonstrate so much around their necks and hanging them with it to show just how truly thankful I am, becoming someone else's property.

It is very difficult telling inquiring minds about those particularly harsh moments when I found myself being punished yet again for one of the myriad offenses I was charged with committing. I came to despise not only the family I was sent to live with, but also the very individuals who condemned me to live out this life without them even present to witness my falling star. With bitter tears running down my cheeks, I laid my head down on the pillow and in my feverish imagination took up a whip and started flogging the whimpering mound of flesh I called 'father.' I cursed this naked specter who filled my mother up with all his hatred for her people and her land and his own choices for getting wrapped up in it. I force fed myself the awful tale of how my mother was simply in the wrong place at the wrong time, and got in my father's way, and so he had his way with her. This bruised apple doesn't fall far from his twisted tree, I convinced myself, that now I must live out my father's legacy.

With the passing years, the wildfires within me are reasonably contained. However, they still smolder deep down with the thought that no one, and yet everyone, is to blame for keeping my father from me I've come to terms that I may never have a name, a picture, nor a hint of a rumor about an old guy living two houses down who's been asking about a son he may have left back in Vietnam. The possibilities of his whereabouts or identity are simply endless. Which means that I, too, am an endless set of possibilities. At least, today I am able to tell the difference between my shadow and his.

On Account of Two Mothers

It's happening again. Just when I start trusting the Night and all its old, twinkling eyes, I feel my fetal-like coil being unspooled, nerve by nerve, and then chopped at the joints and sectioned off into the waiting wings of my two mothers who seem incapable of not yelling at each other. I've been afflicted with this matronly curse ever since life was breathed into me. Their pleading for my attention rings in my ears and turns me into a cornered rat about to eat its tail off inside the galley of a ship full of half-starved mates who also moan for the bickering to end. My genetic mother sits to my right and my homey mother sits to my left, and the same old argument preoccupies their endless days. My sleep is a phantom who laughs from inside the bedroom closet

just as I've become relaxed enough to float out into a
sea of slumber.

My genetic mother questions my homey mother as
to why an odor of butter and baked potatoes emanates
from me all the time. In response, my homey mother
accuses my genetic mother of wanting me to remain
submerged in a clotted stench of fish scales and
sweat. My genetic mother crosses her thin, brown
arms and huffs about how ignorant I am of classic
Vietnamese poetry and folk songs about my people's
origins and triumphs. She is equally saddened by the
fact that I still do not know how to answer her in
Vietnamese when she calls me in her dreams. My
homey mother crosses her freckled, pale arms, and
chides her for giving birth to me in a crowded flat
where two of her brothers were hardened guerrilla
mercenaries who wouldn't have given a second
thought to throwing me out with the bathwater when
they saw my American eyes staring back at them. If
my genetic mother had really wanted me to speak
Vietnamese and recite nationalist poems, then she
would have found a way to keep me and raise me
without regrets instead of just handing me over to my
half-blind poor grandmother and skipping town to do
every Tom, Dick, and Harry who arrived on base.

This tawdry insinuation sets off my genetic
mother. She tears into my homey mother and accuses
her of being contemptuous of her existence and
ignorant of the actual circumstances of her life in
Vietnam. She laments how nobody has ever bothered
to ask her about how she met my father and how he
convinced her that she had the only key to his heart.
There was love before there was fear, my genetic
mother wistfully remembers. My father promised her

that he'd bring her back with him once he finished up his last three months of his tour. No one could tell her why he never returned for her.

The lull between the pointless diatribes ends when my genetic mother suddenly gains her composure and warns my homey mother to stop putting lies in my head. There is no truth behind the rumor that she died giving birth to me nor to the lie that she never wanted me in the first place. Her voice slightly cracks when she yells, "What does an uptight, Midwest farm girl know about life anyway?!" My homey mother jabs her chubby finger at my genetic mother and screams, "What does an uneducated, manipulative Vietnamese city girl know about anything since you're already dead to your son?!"

That's the last straw. My ears are bursting red, aflame with embarrassment for both of them. I throw off my blanket, get out of bed, and quickly put on my sweatshirt and pull on my sweatpants. I need to walk out off this apartment and onto the street where I can glance at people eating ice cream or overhear a sweet conversation about picking up a dog from the groomer, excited and relieved at being reunited with its owner.

I make myself deaf to the shrieking of my two mothers, each one grabbing at me, pulling me into her upteenth stage of grief. No matter what age I'm at I feel the shame of their self-sacrificial love being foisted upon me, forcing me into a mold of a more sympathetic person who will recognize their unique plight. Ultimately, each of their assertion of authority over my life turns me against them. To regain a sense of balance and convince myself of my ability to exercise free will, I do the opposite of what is expected of me. There is no honor in being owned by someone or owning up to anything because someone thinks you should. So, I tell both my mothers, unequivocally, that I belong to neither of them. I am no one's son, despite whoever gave birth to me or took me in. I resolve that I'll always remain a burden.

On that point, there is no argument.

Muted Rage

Kids used to accuse me of being Bruce Lee, as if he were some shiftless, buck-toothed coolie in an old-time photograph begging for a bowl of stale rice. But I didn't have the cutting words at hand to deflect those kids' derogatory remarks. If I had only known then what I know now, that Bruce Lee and I shared the same skin tone, the same black hair and the same inner sense of invincibility. Whenever I found myself to be the only one in a circling, menacing group, I only wanted to be untouchable.

Racism ceased to be an abstraction on one particular day in elementary school when a friend and I were goofing around on this geodesic playground apparatus and some white kid above us decided to smart off by calling my friend a "nigger". Before the kid knew what hit him, both of us grabbed his shirt and started to pull him into the bars. He started crying and threatening to sue us because his father was a lawyer when a teacher ran over, hearing all the ruckus. As the teacher wedged herself in between us, we shouted back, "Go ahead white boy, you got what you deserved!"

Life became even more dicey when this kid and his brother, who lived at the end of the street, taunted me every morning on the school bus no matter where I sat. Eventually, I learned that no matter how small I tried to make myself in the seat, the younger brother would pick me out and box my ears with all his Chinaman jokes. On the ride back home he and his brother would rehash them just for me in case I forgot I wasn't some run-of-the-mill white boy with freckles. The breaking point came when one morning the little brother turned around in his seat and pulled the corner of his eyes to the side and announced, "Hey look, I'm a chink just like you!" Without warning, I swung my fist and connected square with the front of his face. By the time his big brother ripped me off of him, his nose had become a snot bubble. As soon as the bus driver parked the bus at school, I was promptly sent to the principal's office. My parents were called in for a little conference, but I refused to explain my actions. Suffice it to say, I spent a quarter of my elementary school days waiting to be called into the principal's office.

After one particularly unrelenting day of being taunted at school, I took my bike out from the garage and rode around the housing track behind my house. In my right pocket I had a handful of gravel that I scooped up from the side of the road. Checking to see if anyone was around I tossed the rocks liberally into other people's front lawns, hoping that one day all the fathers would be out mowing their precious lawns and with one terrific crack, the mowers' blades would scrape against the stones, causing the engines to shudder to a stop all at once. If my pride was going to be bombarded by their kids each day, then their own vain suburban landscaping projects deserved to be suspended until further notice.

I was boiling and melting at the same time inside. I second-guessed myself each morning I woke up. Preparing for school was like suiting up to go off into a psychological war zone. The non-status I had cultivated among my peers caused me to become withdrawn and highly suspicious of any overture of friendliness that rarely came my way. I figured that since I was being treated as a good-for-nothing, then nothing good would come from trying to connect with others. Once in a while, my mother still will recount the story of how I had barely uttered a single word during a whole school year. I was left speechless. I marked myself absent.

I don't remember my parents ever intervening on my behalf or taking much of an interest in what was going on. Perhaps they did ask, but I was so shell-shocked by the persistent bullying that I cemented the presumption in my mind that no one could see what I had seen. Not only was I an outsider to the other kids, I was outside my parents' purview too. I stopped listening to them; I stopped caring. Since trust was in such short supply, I took myself out of social situations a lot. I was alone to think the unthinkable and sometimes do the unthinkable.

When I was around 9, my parents bought a liver-spotted Dalmatian puppy for me and my two sisters. It was cute as a button and everyone adored it, except me. I tortured that dog. I used a hammer, I used rocks, I used my foot, I used my fists, and I even took a butcher knife and held it to the dog's smooth coat and gently poked it in the ribs. I wanted it to hate me like I hated everyone and everything around me. It gradually became uncontrollable, mean and unpredictable, like me. One summer afternoon, the dog sank her teeth into a neighbor's hand. It just snapped for some reason. I wasn't there to witness this loss of control, this primal reaction to a perceived imminent external threat. I was probably off kicking something down or burning something up. My sister cried her eyes out when our Dad hauled the dog off to the pound the next day.

Shame sat with me on my bed for quite a while that day. I was alone again to sort things out in silence, and justify my value, my existence.

Bruce Lee could've kicked and punched me all day long, but I'd keep on glaring at him, as if he were the only human being in the world who owed me an explanation for why I had become who I was. He died the same year I was born.

Reconstruct

The country of Vietnam became a figment of my imagination. It was a hot air balloon, floating high above a lonesome weathered, green field until it was just a speck, out of sight, out of mind. The North American continent came to dominate my mind's map while I was being taught to see myself as a proud participant in a grand struggle for American cultural and economic supremacy. I saluted only one flag and I pledged allegiance to only one nation every morning in home room. These rote habits drilled into me the message that the only identity I was to accept and present to the public was: "Kevin Keith Allen," eldest son to "Robert" and "Evalyn."

However, this nationalist veneer kept peeling away, layer upon layer, after every unsolicited probe of my foreign origins or unceremonious rejection from a peer group in which I thought I had a right to belong. I turned inward and thought of myself as just some passed-over gift under a global Christmas tree.

Or I looked down on myself as a lone conch shell who was picked up and taken across international time zones to be displayed on the kitchen table of a two-story rambler in a western New York suburb. The call of my birthplace began rushing and abating in my inner ear. I could feel the lunging surf wash over the grains of sand, its natural swish-swash cycle calming me down and lulling me to sleep under many a restless night.

My young soul leapt from island to island, between joy and forgetfulness, and I dared not look down. I didn't want to come down to find myself face to face with what lie hidden beneath the clouds. When I got holed up in some kind of turmoil that left me with only myself to blame, my creators, my parents, awoke inside of me and swelled my breast to speak:

Mother.

Father.

"Who am I?"

"Why did you leave me?"

"Why did they take me away from you?"
 "Are you even there?"

Both a boiling frustration and a deepening depression seemed to be making choices for me or taking away choices that forced me to crawl after them. I doubted my existence and convinced myself that if I up and left, never to be heard from again, no one would come looking for me anyway. These were the moments when I would sit on the edge the bed, close to tears, and run through the list of all the instruments at my disposal that could bring forth my demise: scissors, belts, pills, Dad's hunting rifle.

These were the languishing times when I imagined looking up at my parents' tall, serene figures pointing out toward the sea. A distant rumor would appear like a cork on the vast horizon. But coming into view, closer and closer, the water would turn red and force the graying fish to jump over waves and make way for the rotting, stinking body of a nation-state that had long ago been a bellwether for the U.S.'s global anti-communist campaign.

In its death throes, from 1973 to 1975, the Republic of Vietnam hemorrhaged thousands of its citizens who were dispersed to many other nations under perilous conditions. I was one of those who was abruptly released, although I have no memory of my birth place, nor of fleeing it. Like so many refugees who left behind everything they had known, I count myself as one of the Republic of Vietnam's citizens, one of its sons, for however brief a period in history it was. It is something I can truly say I was a part of, that I belong to, no matter what anyone would try to argue to the contrary.

In an essay I had published in an alternative magazine, I tried to pinpoint the most convincing reason for my existence on this planet:

"I am undeniably tied to this war, intimate with it, in fact. I am the biological outcome of two bodies that met on a certain day, in a certain year, in the Republic of Vietnam, during a war that took them from me before I could remember their voices, what they smelled like and what their names were. The only comfort I take from their absence is that I believe I was picked to survive in order to bear witness to the futility of a war that wiped them off the face of the earth."

As I stand on this beaten shore, watching a pod of whales breach the surface, I steel myself to wade into the murky facts and collect tear-soaked evidence that will lay bare the inscrutible death of my country of birth.

It may not be cathartic.

It may very well be all consuming.

But, perhaps it could reveal a course I haven't yet taken.

Poster Boy

My uncle wore the thick stench of beer on his breath again. He and his family were visiting us from Montana. Unbeknownst to me, after finishing up in the bathroom, he had wandered over to the doorway of my bedroom. I met him there by chance because I was either already heading to my room to escape the boredom of idle chatter or wanting to get something out of it to show my cousins. When my uncle noticed me coming up behind him, he turned to face me and pointed at the poster of Malcolm X on the wall above my bed and declared in a puff of stale alcoholic breath, "You know, that guy was a racist. Yeah, he didn't like people like us." When he said "us", he jabbed his reddish thumb at his chest and then at mine.

My uncle looked at me with his glassy, blood-shot eyes, seeing if I comprehended what he'd just said and then slowly elbowed his way past me. I watched him weave his way gently down the hallway toward the kitchen where he opened the fridge to grab his last beer for the afternoon. I turned and looked at the large poster of Malcolm X and clenched my teeth. Without any recourse, I knew I had been rendered silent once again. My uncle's tipsy remark was yet another unsolicited opinion placed on my doorstep, hastily wrapped, and tick-tick-ticking.

Growing up in a White family and being considered "White" by everyone in my immediate surroundings, in spite of my non-conformance features, afforded me specific entitlements and privileges. My adoptive parents carved out a niche for me in which their family and friends could dote on me and admire my progressive assimilation into their community. Despite this upbringing, my accumulated experience told me that these advantages could be thrown to the wind and I would be interrogated once I stepped outside my familial cocoon. The "real world" would deal significant blows to my sense of security within my family and community every time bigotry, racism and discrimination set their sights on my perceived ethnicity.

During these formative years I started to look at myself from the outside in and gained a better understanding of what it meant to be "race conscious."

In my primary and secondary years of education, teachers presented history as something that happened in the past and the past is what you're supposed to put behind you. Case in point: Schools across the country have canonized Martin Luther King, Jr.'s "I Have A Dream" speech to the exclusion of most of his other important speeches and writings that could provide context to that momentous occasion on the steps of the Lincoln Memorial. My teachers usually showed a video of King's iconic speech to us and told us a convincing tale about how all the appropriate civil rights laws have been passed after all the peaceful, non-violent mass protests took place in the South (and only south of the Mason-Dixon line), and racism and prejudice had been vanquished forever more. But the required reading versions of history didn't cut it for me because the more I read on my own the less I depended on the official version of American history. I long suspected I had to look for and examine many versions of history and weigh one against the other in the face of ever-growing factual evidence. It was the only way to catch a glimpse of the truth behind the lies. This led me to come across *The Autobiography of Malcolm X* in the school library when I was 17. His story awakened my young mind to a seminal figure who tore off the gilded surface of America for anyone curious enough to look under the hood of the Land of the Free and to see the grime and dirt, and all its moving parts.

I read the entire book in about two weeks. The words, the ideas, the life experience contained within those pages were like a breath of fresh air in my stale suburban enclave. Malcolm went from a self-hating and self-pitying "nigga" who felt he had nothing to live for to a man who finally found his calling in life. What impressed me the most was his will to serve a higher purpose and to rouse Black Americans, as well as other oppressed people of color, from their passive slumber and embolden them to demand to be seen in the same dignified light as White Americans and to pursue their liberation from White supremacy "by any means necessary."

Reading about Malcolm X's travails as a child and a young man in Nebraska and then in Boston and New York, as well as his developing and evolving convictions, spoke to my own fledgling beliefs about personal accountability and self-worth. The racism and dehumanization that Malcolm X experienced as a young man validated my casual observations of prejudice and racism while living in a predominately White suburb in western New York.

Malcolm X's words and ideas taught me what a functioning democracy is supposed to offer its citizens and what it means to want and seek justice within and without the rule of law. The legitimacy and moral weight of a democratic government lie in how it treats its minority populations and its most vulnerable members. If the government, with the majority's support, excludes, exploits and dehumanizes those outside of the sanctioned power core, then it begs the question whether or not those minority populations have any responsibility in upholding said government. It's a fundamental debate that is embedded in our national psyche and continues to ground our political culture.

Because of my readings of *The Autobiography of Malcolm X*, as well as his collected speeches (i.e., *Malcolm X: The Last Speeches* and *Malcolm X Talks To Young People: Speeches in the United States, Britain, and Africa*), I was performing my own form of redress for ignoring the downtrodden voices of the past and naively accepting what I had internalized from my inner circles as well as society at large. I wanted to rebel against know-nothing-ism and willful ignorance and against White Flight righteousness and self-imposed segregation. Instead of being comfortable with thoughts and opinions that I had been told to believe, I looked beyond my own backyard and started to ask uncomfortable questions. As I was to find out halfway into my senior year of high school, this existential rebellion couldn't have come at a better time. The more I read, the more my comprehension of race relations in the United States made great strides as I connected the dots between past and present government policies that encoded and enforced racial discrimination at all levels of civic life. I soon began to see for myself that something was just not right whenever I tried to match American ideals with actual practices.

When video of the repeated beating of Rodney King in Los Angeles by several police officers was broadcast nationally to a stunned viewership, it confirmed much of my comprehension of what Malcolm X had been criticizing about race relations in America.

When I first watched that nondescript figure on TV struggling on the ground while two policemen were wailing on his chest and legs mercilessly, I wanted to reach through the screen and block those body blows. The victim, Rodney King, was obviously frightened and disoriented and trying to muster as much energy as possible to escape the nightsticks and taser cables trying to immobilize his body. As the weeks and months went by after that infamous video had been broadcast, the words of Malcolm X rang out loud and clear in my head, and I knew I could never go back to the somnolence of suburbia.

The riots that erupted in south central Los Angeles in April 1992 touched off conflagrations in other cities around the country, including my hometown, Rochester, NY. Even after the prosecution rested its case and clarity had been provided as to what exactly happened on that frightful night, it enraged me, as well as any other sensible and decent American, that the policemen who were caught on video committing such an egregious overreach of their power were acquitted and legally absolved of any guilt. When I first heard the breaking news on TV, my whole body felt like screaming and my parents were worried about me when they saw me punching the air as I marched to my bedroom. Malcolm X's anger at those who would deny any person's struggle for justice was demonstrably reflected in my feelings that day. It felt liberating to me to know that I was not alone in wanting to hold my fellow countrymen to a higher standard of citizenship and humanity.

To this day, I consider Malcolm X to be one of my personal heroes. Although I don't have many deeply held convictions, one of them is echoed in the words

Malcolm once said: "I am not a racist. I am against every form of racism and segregation, every form of discrimination. I believe in human beings, and that all human beings should be respected as such, regardless of their color."

This is a quote I wish I could've repeated to my uncle and explained to him the reason it held so much meaning for me.

De Profundis

In the photo lies an infant
toothpick limbs at his side,
motionless, mouth agape.

Yellowing paper ages his skin and leaves him
transparent underneath the afterglow
of a photographer's flashbulb.

The sisters named him.

Up from the depths,
he called from the back of a bus
with no arms curled under him.
The nurses thought he'd never live past a week.
But when his sores healed and the clouds in his eyes
parted,
he posed for the camera on the floor of the
orphanage,
plump cheeks laughing.
 One more child flown out of the carcass of civil war.
A life saved to memorialize those who perished
in the wind above the coast.

The above poem was my first attempt at addressing adoption in all its complexities. I never figured that I'd ever write a poem let alone one about adoption. From the outside, the fact that I was born to one set of parents and then uprooted and sent to live with a different set of parents would have been an obvious writing prompt from anyone else's perspective. However, from the tundra of my interior, the upheaval and drama of my very first moments on this planet were off limits to my beginner's writing hand. Call it an inferiority complex, but for the longest time I didn't believe my story had a strong enough voice to even warrant a period on paper. Furthermore, knowing that I was a true orphan actually orphaned me from my own recollections and feelings about what it was like to live as a child of color, from a foreign country, in a Catholic-oriented White household smack-dab in suburbia. My "De Profundis" poem is certainly about another child, but it tangentially refers to my own resurrected insights as a mixed-race Vietnamese person who was adopted by a heterosexual White American couple.

The origin of my poem's title lies in a book called *Turn My Eyes Away*. It's a slightly oversized hardcover book containing photographs, stories and quotations compiled by Rosemary Taylor, an Australian and a prominent figure in establishing orphanages in South Vietnam during the War. Perhaps due to its exposure to the elements in my childhood house, the book closely resembles a yellowing dossier. She dedicated the book to the orphans and their caretakers who perished on the first official Operation Babylift flight in April 1975. My parents were given the book, I believe, when they adopted my younger sister. As a youngster, I used to look through the book without comprehending its subject matter or being told the background story of why my parents stuffed it alongside all their other reference books on a shelf in their entertainment center next to the TV in the basement. I was oblivious to the book's intent and the history it could have imparted to me about the country in which I was born. In my developing brain, I thought I was just looking at some strange kids who needed to be fed and clothed. It never occurred to me that I was living out of context, not even cognizant that my own story was written in those pages.

Back in 1999, during a personal reclamation project I initiated on behalf of myself, when it was readily apparent that I was increasingly distancing myself from the community that had housed me, I retrieved *Turn My Eyes Away* from the bookshelf it had sat on for so many years and put it on the night table by my bed. Every time my eyes wandered over to the black-and-white photograph of the teary-eyed cherub on the front cover I hesitated to open it. I hate being manipulated to emote on cue. It always seems that an invisible hand guides me to advance my agenda. So, one night I took another look at that book cover and took a deep breath. I got comfortable on the bed and started reading each section intently, familiarizing myself with the names of the Westerners, identified by Ms. Taylor, as being seminal in leading the charge to set up religious-inspired orphanages and ultimately organizing the effort to collect and fly out thousands of infants and older children to countries like Australia, the U.S.,

England and Germany for the purposes of adoption. I looked at every child in each photo and read each caption. When I came across the photos of the crash of the C5-A cargo plane with the blackened smoke and wet wind that blanketed the nondescript rice paddy, I was both saddened and outraged that such a thing happened. It jumbled my concept of sheer accident, destiny and simple human failing. I wanted to know for sure that all the kids who died were spoken for and not just tallied up on a DOD stats sheet as "MIA." As much as *Turn My Eyes Away* produced innate pity and sadness inside of me, it left me even more critical of what I had been told all along about the history and rationale of the American war effort in my country of birth.

Although *Turn My Eyes Away* produced a lot of unexpected, but genuine, feelings in me, I didn't know where to take them to be processed or how to examine their worth or validity. I guess that's the main reason I turned to the craft of poetry. To me, the most shocking photo in the book took up two pages. It showed an emaciated boy lying in a crib with dark boils all over his skin, sporting white bandages wrapped around his hands and around the crown of his head. His wide-open eyes betrayed confusion, shock and the fear of facing an uncertain future. My sympathies weren't prepared for the image I would see when I turned the page. I came face to face with the photo of a healthy, plump infant with a dark tuft of hair sticking straight up, sitting straight up and laughing. According to the caption, this was, amazingly, the same boy a couple months later, after he was properly fed and cared for. His caretakers, lovingly gave him the nickname 'De Profundis,' Latin for "up from the depths."

The connotation of resurrection, or rebirth, attached to the name 'De Profundis' is a pointed reminder that religious activism galvanized many a volunteer to travel to South Vietnam and lend their hearts and energy after they read about, or saw on TV news broadcasts, the children living in over-crowded orphanages. The righteousness and sense of benevolence these volunteers worked under to uplift and try to save the impoverished and forlorn children both galled me and made me react indignantly. For *Turn My Eyes Away* is a testament to the assumed humanism, grace and selflessness of the Westerner, none of which is reserved for the Vietnamese nor their offspring. The photos of the children and the narratives that accompany them prove fundamental in establishing the White upper hand that is invariably accepted. To not do so would inevitably rain down accusations of ingratitude and disloyalty.

'De Profundis' is counted as a blessing. By extension, all of us adopted from Vietnam are meant to have blessed the homes and families that took us in, as well as the countries that provided us cover. For many that was the only message imparted to us if we ever asked about our origins. In my own way, the poem that started this whole essay was meant not as a betrayal of the savior message, but as a note to append to it. The note being that there is a much bigger truth involved behind my and De Profundis' life. That we have been uniquely intertwined in the paradox of human compassion and cruelty.

Help Now, Cry Later

At the close of the Vietnam War, hundreds of Vietnamese children under the jurisdiction of Western relief agencies and religious-focused orphanages, as well as any other child that was handed to them or was picked up off the street, were flown out of South Vietnam and placed with adoptive parents in Western countries under the umbrella of the U.S. government's project "Operation Babylift" (hereafter initialized "OBL"). By the time the Vietnam War officially ended on April 30, 1975, approximately 3,000 infants and young children were taken out of the war-torn country for the purpose of adoption. Each time the month of April approaches, the anniversary of this singular event is celebrated, and I believe it is worth re-examining because, to this day, most Westerners, especially Americans, consider OBL to be "the one good thing that came out of the war."

As the war was being waged in South Vietnam, many Americans read about hapless, homeless and traumatized children in the newspaper and saw their desperate little faces on the evening news. Quite a few believed they had a moral responsibility to take care of those less fortunate and open their hearts and homes to the children of a war that they conveniently forgot their country had escalated. Along with this newfound evangelism, the implied politicized message was that Americans were more moral than those "godless communists", aka the Vietnamese, and that only Americans could provide an exponentially better outcome to these young castaways. Under the protection of the U.S. military and with the support of

countless donations, several religious groups
established orphanages that inadvertently, but no less
effectively, took the place of indigenous methods and
solutions for child welfare. With so much of South
Vietnam overwhelmed by the casualties of war,
enterprising "good Samaritans" took up the mantle of
healer and savior.

A rarely acknowledged correlation between the
war and adoption is that the longer the U.S. military
and civilian personnel stayed in South Vietnam, the
more prostitution and intermarriage produced
children of mixed race — the Amerasians — many of
whom were orphaned or abandoned. The media
portrayed Amerasians as caged animals who were
unwanted by their unfeeling mothers and Missing-in-
Action fathers. In order to soothe their conscience and
fulfill a sense of obligation to those fathered by their
countrymen, Americans advocated for the adoption of
Amerasians. Unintentional or not, the adopting out of
Amerasian children became the Trojan Horse for
institutionalizing international adoption across the
board.

The protagonists of Operation Babylift are
credited with saving thousands of children who
otherwise would have grown up in a postwar
communist dictatorship where food shortages and
other deprivations would have condemned them to
lifelong servitude or certain death. Left out of this
narrative is that the American government propped up
corrupt dictatorial regimes in South Vietnam one after
the other that pilfered and siphoned off much foreign
aid into their own international bank accounts. What
also goes unmentioned is the fact that over six million
tons of bombs fell on a country roughly the size of

New Mexico during the 10 years of American
involvement in the war which directly contributed to
so many children being orphaned and made available
for adoption in the first place. In my opinion, it is not
a far reach to interpret OBL as having become a
redundant closed-loop system of mourning,
remembrance, gratitude and redemption. It is
continually celebrated as an unprecedented unilateral
humanitarian gesture. Ironically, by remembering
OBL in such a way it encourages the so-called "war
waifs" to forget the causes and effects of the Vietnam
War and leaves unexamined their own adoption
stories that were virtually gift-wrapped and handed to
them.

To this day, first generation Vietnamese adoptees
are generally referred to as 'war orphans' in the
media and by people they encounter on a daily basis,
as if it were a self-applied term of endearment. The
main assumption is that they were rescued from a
tragic past and handed a hopeful future. The public
was reassured that these children were not going to
look back and puzzle together the facts behind their
orphan status.

Granted, I was adopted from Vietnam several
months before Operation Babylift occurred, but I still
feel compelled to question the historical
interpretations of the Vietnam War, as well as other
people's motives and methods for removing me and
my contemporaries from our birth country. The
strange irony remains a dark truth that in order for
many of us Vietnamese adoptees to have gained our
second family, we had to lose our first. The following
lines from a poem of mine encapsulate my conflicted

feelings on the legacy of being transported from one
life to another:

At the age of six, grandma took me to the zoo,
and when it came time to leave I didn't want to
get back in the car because the lions reminded me
of the cage back home, except the one back home
opened up once in a while to let me see the new
neighbors moving into new houses
in what used to be our new backyard.

Slip of the Tongue

From the time I could read, I had always been a
student of history, like a botanist to the shapes of
leaves or an oceanographer to the flow of currents.
War, militarization and propaganda were the subjects
I inevitably gravitated towards. Momentous battles
laid out in coffee table books fascinated me and I
wanted to know more about the causes of such
conflicts, how weapons technology evolved and who
the victors and the vanquished were. Knowing that I
was the product of a war myself, I didn't consider my
interest in war's manifestations to be morbid at all. To
learn about how wars were initiated, prosecuted and
brought to a close only clarified my own station in the
world.

As my mind matured and my consciousness
deepened, I began reading more complex works on
history and politics. This made me frequently
question myself and other people about how war
affects the way we keep perceiving the world, and
each other, in black and white. Some of my core

questions have become so increasingly complex or too convoluted that it has become nearly impossible to fit in any easy answers. That said, I've come to the sobering conclusion that war is humankind's lasting inheritance.

Whenever the idea of starting a family came to mind or was the topic of discussion, from the very start I objected to bringing a child into this world. My knowledge from all the reading I had done and after much contemplation on my own beginnings told me that the bombing of bloodlines is the inevitable result of using our scientific knowledge and technical acumen to aggressively gain an advantage over perceived enemies. Our rationale for waging war, or at least supporting it in far flung regions of the world, rests on blind faith, superstition and age-old nationalist myths that create the belief there are people who need to pay the price for being non-believers and refusing to follow in the path of our Manifest Destiny. This mentality minimizes the furtherance of mutual aid and the repairing of rifts between societies, all in order to advance a cynical agenda that will benefit only the group to which we feel most attached.

Thus, in my judgment, having a child of my own would only add to the cacophony of people vying for limited resources and livable space. The addition of another human is not a hopeful sign; it's an act of domination. Envy, selfishness and brutishness incubate within expansive human populations and lead to murderous friction between communities and individuals — individuals who were once doted on for their cute looks and precocious antics. However, children do not stay children forever, and they become either the hapless victims of war or, conversely, its conniving perpetrators.

Although being adopted and whisked away from a grueling war in Southeast Asia was a fortuitous opportunity for me to live a life more positive, I have always felt a subversive history lurking behind the passport that identifies me as a full-fledged citizen of the United States of America. This alterna-story tells the tale of a boy living a life just as happily and successfully in Vietnam, as in any other random Western country. If not for random acts of kindness, my life could have ended unceremoniously before it even began. If life has taught me anything by now, it is that nothing truly follows a straight line and ends in a foregone conclusion.

I've known for a long time that I would never relish re-telling any child of mine about how I was taken in by another family, branded with a new name and told to go play outside as if nothing prior to my arrival in the U.S. had happened. I especially wanted to avoid encountering the vision of any child of mine watching his daddy kneeling at the edge of a gaping ditch, looking in vain for a family tree that had long since been uprooted and turned to pulp. I have made the steadfast choice not to use a child to fill in the absence of blood relatives in my life. Although I have no documentation of what my parents looked like, every time I look in the mirror I'm essentially looking back at them. Their genes are the building blocks that formed my physical presence that stands before them now.

When my parents left life's stage, they took with them all the knowledge of their ancestors — my ancestors. Empty picture frames on my life's walls were replaced with another set of parents who filled them in with their own childhoods and their own relatives, who bore no resemblance to me. Living with such grievous loss underscored for me that there was no way for me, in good conscience, to create an artificial branch and try grafting it onto a family tree that I just couldn't claim.

Like my birthparents, I will leave this planet with no trace. I will not be leaving behind a living legacy; I do not need to see a part of me in anyone else; I do not need to validate my social position by raising a prodigal son or daughter. Any ambition to make my mark on the world by siring an heir to carry my good name does not appeal to me. It is truly liberating to know that there is no shame in cutting all ties and drifting away when the time comes.

I slipped into this world, and I will slip out of it.

Dish

From the beginning I've felt as if I've been living in opposition to the world at large. There seemed to be just no way I could rightfully feel at peace in the tiny spot that had been pushed aside for me to occupy. I've never particularly enjoyed revealing how adoption has played such an outsized role in my origins as a human being. It has much to do with me reducing the act of adoption to a simple transaction involving my body being "given up" and then "taken in" like a second-hand trinket at a local flea market. As long as this metaphor was causing confusion inside my brain about my own social worth, I remained susceptible to allowing other people's misconceptions about adoption subsume my will to think for myself.

When I first started opening myself up and flipping through the blank pages of my own life in 1999, I felt both a piercing curiosity and wonderful empowerment. No longer needing to hide behind the insular small-town rites I once felt I had to abide by, I wondered how many other people were like me, an adult adoptee of Vietnamese descent. Because the 25th anniversary of the end of the Vietnam/American War was being celebrated at the time, I found myself awash in news articles about Vietnamese adoptees living their lives in other states like Colorado, California and New Jersey, and even in other parts of the world like Australia, Germany and England. It amazed me, the plethora of faces and stories similar to mine, because, other than my sister, who was also adopted from Vietnam, I had not been in contact with others who shared a similar immigration timeline as mine.

In late 2000, my life seemed to change all at once when my fingers casually typed in "Vietnamese adoptees" in Yahoo's search engine. A website for an organization called "Vietnamese Adoptee Network" appeared. I clicked on its link and carefully announced myself to the group on its bulletin board. Almost immediately I was inundated with messages from numerous strangers breathlessly revealing their experiences and opinions as adopted persons from the old South Vietnam and urging me to join in and share my experience. A strong comradery would blossom and quick affinities were made between me and so many people onscreen that I could hardly tell them apart. It was hard not to get carried away by the mutual positivity of it all because it was new and it was what I was looking for all this time, feeling as though I was uniquely strange and utterly alone.

Over the past 17 years I can say, with a large body of experience behind me, that the dynamic we adult adoptees have created and maintained, the establishment of friendships made both online and in real life, and the evolution of our maturity and worldviews through the years, we remain together as much as we remain disparate. The early internet and relatively new social platforms, like Facebook, have contributed enormously to establishing and pushing our unique interests into the limelight within policy and academic circles, and major and minor artistic venues, helping us realize our strength in numbers and undaunted tenacity. But also I've personally experienced the all-too-human fallback of cliquishness and egotism rending groups and organizations apart when they've gone untended or, even worse, instituted without a hint of irony whatsoever. All things considered, I've learned that even though we adult Vietnamese adoptees may share a common ethnicity and brief history together, and that we may be able to communicate on an intuitive level about what it means to be adopted, these commonalities cannot replace the fact that we are each individuals with very different needs, wants and ambitions.

When all is said and done, I continue on being whomever I'm supposed to be. But, whenever I'm asked about my origins and I let go that I was adopted, I'm always painfully aware of the many faces I struggle to simultaneously reveal and to conceal. It's that feeling of "two steps forward, one step back" defining the direction of my life.

What I always brace for, after the question is asked, is the common reaction from the inquirer, usually a combination of unreserved sadness, as if I had told them I just came from the doctor's office and I only have two weeks to live, and simpering pity, or even condolences, which make the air between us even more awkward. Furthermore, when I follow up with the story about being adopted from Vietnam during the War, it never fails that I'm told, in a variety of amusing ways, that I must feel lucky I wasn't left there to die and that I must really appreciate living in the U.S. because of all the rainbows, unicorns and Hershey chocolate bars that live here. Then there's always the expectation that I will share in this person's platitudes and head-patting because such ignorance and arrogance have always been rewarded with a blush and a smile. It's been ingrained in me since childhood that I'm supposed to always accept such presumptuousness with grace and a (fake) smile. However, being older and understanding better the ways of the world's machinations, I've become less and less accommodating toward others' received wisdom about how I should view my life on their terms. Now I tend to place their preconceptions under the microscope and then tell them where to go directly if they disagree with my analysis.

Admittedly, I'm still uncertain how I'm supposed to approach the realities and legacies of adoption completely on my own terms. Even before I could talk I've told myself that my family tree has long since been burned to the ground, and the empty pages in my book are ripe for exploitation of wishful thinking and misguided fantasies. My conception and birth are as real as the air I draw in every single day, but beyond that I am the only evidence that my parents had ever existed on this planet. Others may be persuaded that I'm too serious, too cynical or too indifferent because my past is unsettled and the facts of my life could swiftly shift into the realm of fiction.

In the end, I can only offer this peek into the bittersweet irony of growing up adopted in an interracial family. It is the distinct memory of my sister and I riding in the car with my parents about to cross the Canadian border, and my mother hastily taking out my and my sister's naturalization papers from the glove compartment. The documents had been slipped into plastic sleeves and secured neatly in musty black leather protectors. While idling in line before reaching the guard booth, my parents coached my sister and me to say, "Yes," when we were asked whether or not we are American citizens and that, "Yes," the people in the front seat of the car are our actual parents. All this hand-wringing seemed amusing to me because it was illogical in my child's mind to have to verify to a perfect stranger what I had always taken for granted to be quite obvious in my household. In spite of that, I'll have to remind myself that there will always be a disjuncture between how I see myself and how others view me within the panopticon of daily life.

I Might Be Hawai'ian

When I landed in Honolulu, Hawai'i to attend the Asian Adult Adoptee Gathering & Film Festival in October 2008, my first objective was to head to those fabled beaches that had been reflected in my mind's eye after so many years of being inculcated with the mainland's fantasies of those islands. It is my belief that when I was born a tropical hormone flowed inside my blood stream, making me pine for salty blue waters and cracked coconuts. When the #19 bus arrived at the airport, I heaved my two full backpacks onto my back and walked into the air-conditioned cabin. Luckily, I got a window seat so I could stare out at the scenery streaking by. As the bus wound through its elongated route, I marveled in my head at the various people boarding and exiting the bus. I have a bad habit of staring, so I was probably more than a little conspicuous when I took in the many visages of Hawai'i. Old and young, men and women, walked, hobbled and skipped by my tan, hairy legs and I suddenly got an eerie feeling that I may very well be looking at one of my own relatives.

As crazy as it sounded to me, and as large as the odds were, it was not a completely irrational suspicion. My being of mixed race, born in Vietnam and then brought to the U.S. as an infant to be adopted, who carried very little identifying information with him, makes any definitive declaration on my ethnic heritage extremely tenuous at best.

I've only recently acknowledged the difficulty of accepting the typewritten racial identification, "Vietnamese/white," on a piece of paper, possibly from the orphanage I had been residing in. When I consider that Thai, Chinese, Filipino and Korean men, as well as Mien, Hmong and Montangard men, and even Native American and Latino men, participated in combat operations and acted as support personnel during the war in Vietnam, the "Vietnamese/white" parts ascribed to me start to take a back seat. My naturally dark tan skin and ambiguously mixed Asian facial features point in many directions other than the "white" label on that piece of paper. It's anyone's guess nowadays.

My mother could have been anything other than a native Vietnamese. Whenever she comes to mind, I imagine her having been a resident of Hawai'i who took a job as an administrative assistant at any one of the numerous American companies that had contracts with the Pentagon or the old Republic of Vietnam. She, possessing a sense of adventure or being just plain tired of the monotony of the same-ol'-same-ol' on the island, snatched up the opportunity to transfer to an office in Saigon for a year. In contrast to her white co-workers, my mother may have felt very comfortable in the humidity and hustle-and-bustle of brown people, living and dying as they had done for centuries. My mother very well could have dated a handsome Vietnamese man who had swept her off her feet with his natural cordiality and raucous laughter. It is one of millions of possibilities.

At the conference, I had taken part in a panel featuring adoptees of mixed race with four other people. Only after I returned home did it occur to me that each of those four people had been reunited with their first mothers, except for me. Later on at lunch, after the panel had ended, I was fascinated listening to all of them talk about their unique relationships with their first mothers and how these re-connections have developed over the years. I was intrigued, more for the fact that I had resigned myself to the near certainty that I would never come to know who my parents were. For me, it's not a matter of giving up on some kind of hope of finding them, but rather a re-prioritization of focus on things that I would like to achieve within the relatively short lifespan I've been afforded.

The Vietnam War did strange things to people. In my case, it gave me life while possibly sentencing my parents to death. The war's massive carnage and destruction also reduced any possibility of searching for my parents or receiving any kind of credible information on them while, paradoxically, at the same time expanding the possibilities of their whereabouts and identities to near endless proportions.

So, as I sat on that #19 bus, I made believe that a close relative of mine was sitting right across from me and staring right back at my curious face.

In Spirit Only

If you were to ask me what my parents' names are, what they look like or whether you could meet them now, I'd apologize for any disappointment that may arise in you, but I would have to tell you that my existence is the only memento I have of my parents. My physical being is the only evidence I have proving my parents were once alive and, at one time or another, came together on this planet.

The story that was plucked out of thin air and given to me is that my mother was a Vietnamese native and my father an American serviceman, and both of them soon died, and I was given to my destitute grandmother to raise, and she, in turn, gave me up to an orphanage where strangers would give me the care that my grandmother could not provide. Growing up in a suburb of western New York, whenever I looked in the mirror, I would play a little game of dividing up parts of my face and push them to either the Vietnamese side or the Caucasian side. I would guess where my mother's eyes began and where my father's nose ended, or attribute the lack of height to my mother's genes and my curly, wavy hair to my father's genes. It became habitual, pulling myself apart and attempting to rebuild myself based on whichever mood I found myself in. However, there was always that stigma of simply being the offspring of two people I will never know, and yet with whom I remain intimately familiar.

Pictures to piece together my parents' lives in order to put mine into perspective would show me just how much I look like them. I could verify at least that I look more like one or the other. I could smile and think, "So that's where I got my hair from." Photos would act as a bridge to re-connect me to two people who gave me life. Without a photo album to open and point to pictures of my mom as a teenager or my dad on his first day of school, and the stories that go along with them, compounds the significant feeling of loss. There was always a hurt deep inside me knowing that I was unable to trace myself back to any root structure.

Kids usually want to know what their parents were like when they were younger and what they had done when they were at that age. Not only is this a basic human desire to want to belong to a cohesive, familiar social unit, it's an ancient emotional tool for finding meaning and purpose in one's life. It's only natural that parents would want to pass down stories, like they had passed down their genes, to their children in order to secure their burgeoning identities in an ever-changing world.

Even though my adoptive parents told me some stories from their own lives, which I gladly accepted, I was still left wanting to know the stories that only my birthparents could tell me. I missed knowing how they met and what they had made of themselves once they had gone their separate ways. They could have clued me into which traits or quirks they passed down to me. Absent their voices, I could only go on imagining what my mother and father would say to me if they were here.

When everything is said and done, though, I can either accept all that life has given me and build on it or continue digging down through time until I reach the rich tombs of the people who conceived me in order to claim my birthright. I understand that taking either path could lead to fulfilling discoveries. Given further thought, I could switch between paths depending on which one seems to offer the most promising result at the time. An even more courageous choice would be total transcendence of any fixed pathway and release from destiny's trappings. Be that as it may, wherever I go, my reflection will follow.

Locks of Hair

Dear Mother,

You would be glad to see that I'm alive and doing quite well. But, I can't lie. It has been a struggle to mature into the person I am now. In spite of it, I keep gaining wisdom and I believe I can make a name for myself. Poetry has become my main means of self-expression, and more and more short stories, and essays have been effective means for communicating my point of view. One could say that I'm plotting out my past and future lives under the eyes of the present. It's taken a while, but I'm getting to know the person I was and the person I may become. Right now, I'm doing my best to bear witness and enjoy the life you breathed into me.

Funny story. My first American name wasn't "Kevin," it was "Dominic." I still can't imagine being called 'Dom,' 'Nick' or 'Nicky.' I found this out because Evalyn, my other mom, told me prior to me reading all the documentation she had saved concerning my adoption back in 1974. Evalyn explained to me that she and her husband, Bob, were not the first couple to adopt me. A young couple near Springfield, Missouri had brought me to their home first and took care of me for a couple months until their marriage dissolved. According to the adoption agency's rules, they had to put me back under the care of the agency. I was promptly sent to a foster family somewhere in Colorado, and within a month Evalyn and Bob waited for me to arrive at the airport in Rochester, New York after they had officially adopted me. As I like to humorously point out to

anyone who'd listen, I had gone through three names
— Nguyen Duc Minh, Dominic and Kevin Keith
Allen — before I turned even a year old.

Perhaps it's a bit strange to think this, but I need to
hold onto you in some way. Even though I have no
memory of you, no pictures of you as a girl, as a
woman, and no stories of what you were like, I feel a
connection still. Your presence sounds like a song,
like a woman's voice singing to her child in her arms.
The words I don't understand, but I'm oddly aware
that the song is meant for me. It's hard going through
life admitting to people that I don't know what you
look like and don't know your name, and that in the
end I was simply adopted by a nice American family.
If only I had a picture of you or perhaps at least a
picture of your grave, then that would at least be
definitive proof of your coming and going. And what
if nothing about you materializes? What then? Then I
am your proof. I have to come to terms that all the
proof I need to show people you lived is me, standing
before their eyes..

Saigon, Vietnam is the city where I was born.
Webster, New York is the town where I was raised.
The two probably couldn't be more different from
each other. I want to visit that other part of my life,
the origin of my birth in Vietnam. It's like Mecca to a
Muslim: if you are able bodied and have the means,
you must come back to the source and pay your
respects. Hopefully, such a return will fill a void or
perhaps give me a better understanding of my life. I
will not know until I get there.

My adoptive parents were very happy to receive
me on that November day in 1974. I've looked at the
photos of my reaction as that large group of people

converged to see the new arrival numerous times now. My face was plump and flush. My natural curls looked tousled from uneasy sleep. My eyes were wide with a bit of surprise and awe. I had no idea who was holding me and I didn't know I was being handed over to new parents. It looked like I was in desperate need of an explanation.

People say that I should just get on with my life, as if nothing had happened between you and father, and I was the result. These people generally mean well, and they're not completely wrong. I do question what the use is in pining for someone you cannot see on the other side of a spectrum neither of you are aware of, while life's events and milestones accumulate despite your secret tears. I still do that thing when I lie awake, motionless, after a long sleep. I hum words to myself that I do not understand, but which seem to implore me to return to a land where I'll see you and you'll see me. Until then, I'll live off the time you gave me.

Your Son.

Photos of Us

The hallway on the second floor of the Seattle Center leading to the video presentation room was set up to resemble a hallway in a typical suburban home with several family portraits hanging neatly on the wall. These portraits resembled the ones that many of us have taken a second, or third, look at and asked ourselves, "How do I fit in among these people?" It reminded me of back home when I would stop and stare at my image mixed among photos of relatives, come and gone, and ponder the color contrast readily apparent in my family. I knew I looked different from my parents, but I didn't feel all that different. My facial features and physique looked Asian, but I didn't know what it meant to be Asian. "How can I be so sure of who I am," I would ask myself.

"So, what is your purpose here? Why are you showing all this adoption stuff?" It had taken this brash young man, who seemed to have something to prove to his girlfriend, to shake me out of my agreeable public personae. This guy had demanded a straight answer out of me, an answer I had assumed was self-evident. He made me confront the realization that during that whole weekend I had been asking myself the same two questions, although on mute and in the back of my mind. Unexpectedly, this Vietnamese man provoked me to reflect on the meaning of those two afternoons spent at the Seattle Center.

One reason we, as representatives of Vietnamese Adoptee Network, wanted to put in an appearance at the Tet festival was because we had something to contribute to the notion of being Vietnamese-American. We were born in Vietnam, but the majority of us were raised by Caucasian parents. Because of this family dynamic, our national and ethnic identities often crisscross many social and geopolitical boundaries. It would be too simplistic for us to claim one flat-rate identity over the other because neither of us are simply one or the other.

Debate and conflict can hardly be avoided when it comes to talking about Vietnam and the United States, or even being of Vietnamese descent living in the United States. As adult Vietnamese adoptees, we sit in the crosshairs of many competing agendas. Many people claim that we were spared from living out a terrible existence in a severely impoverished country. Some would have us believe that we should appreciate all that we were given and blindly go about our lives without a care. Some people insist that we should remember Vietnam as our homeland and that each of us must go back to pay our respects. Some people exclaim that we have no perceptible connection to Vietnam and we should just be proud to be Americans. Some of us have been asked why we are here. Perhaps some of us have been told to go back to where we came from.

At first, the issue doesn't seem so complicated because many of us don't feel any different from any other American, and it would be presumptuous for anyone else to question our identity as Americans. Our parents were present when we took our first steps, our relatives celebrated each birthday with us, and we mimicked their accents and picked up some of their mannerisms.

However, as each of us takes the time to look outside ourselves and into our Vietnamese past, we must struggle to comprehend Vietnam as a land, a people, a way of life, and not just as a cuisine, a travel show or a movie. If we truly want to explore that other unrealized side, we must determine how much of ourselves we are willing to invest in identifying with Vietnam and the Vietnamese, with that other history, that other identity. Guilt is a common lingering feeling when we begin to deal with our real or imagined pasts in the shadow of our relatives and friends. Perhaps some people would feel guilty about appearing disloyal or that they are betraying all they know if they become more and more interested in their birth country. Some adoptees may feel guilty if they hold no interest in their Vietnamese heritage. They would question whether they're subconsciously denying a large part of who they are.

The executive director of the organization that produced the Tet in Seattle event compared the Vietnamese adoptee situation to that in which young Vietnamese-Americans find themselves. He said that many of his peers have fought numerous inner battles that dealt with how to interact with people they see on a daily basis, and how they fit into mainstream American society. For many young Vietnamese-Americans they must find their own way of appropriating American mores and culture into their lives without offending their elders, and without ignoring their unique cultural heritage their parents were raised in and carried over to this country. At times, it may seem there is an American team and a Vietnamese team, and each of them continuously questions their players' loyalty or allegiance to the group, as if there were only one correct choice. But this accomplished young professional said that eventually everyone handles these extraordinary social pressures his or her own way. To him, that's what being Vietnamese and American means.

A second important reason why our group had an exhibit at this Vietnamese New Year Festival was because we felt we deserved to be there among our Vietnamese-American brothers and sisters, aunts and uncles, whether any of us felt more Vietnamese or American that day or not. I watched as old and young Vietnamese-Americans perused the reading material and looked and pointed at the photos. I observed the expressions on their faces and tried to listen in on their conversations to glean some insight into what they were thinking when they were looking over our baby pictures. In a subversive fashion, we were re-introducing ourselves to the Vietnamese-American community as a group of people who had been born in Vietnam and then, figuratively speaking, reborn in the United States upon our adoption into American homes. For the longest time both of our communities have been living separate lives, but this festival gave us a great opportunity to come together under one roof and find out how we've been doing all these years.

A couple days after the event, one of the volunteers at our exhibition told me he witnessed something peculiar at the end of our time at the festival. He saw a teenage girl wearing a colorful *ao dai* primping in front of the mirror we had hung on the wall close to the entrance of the lobby to the exhibit. Underneath this mirror read a sign, 'Who Am I?', which caught her attention. After fixing her hair to be just as she wanted it, she said aloud, half to herself and half to whomever was nearby, "Who am I? I'm a Vietnamese girl, of course!" She then gave a cursory glance towards our table, turned quickly on her toe and walked away, satisfied with her answer.

My Re-Emergence

It took me 41 years and four months to return to the city in which I was born in December 1973. Sài Gòn, Việt Nam, is a city that no longer recognizes me as one of its sons because I was raised in a culture of mac-n-cheese and not Bún bò Huế. Nonetheless, I had been psychologically preparing for the moment when I would arrive at Tan Son Nhat International Airport on April 2nd and step on Vietnamese soil and breathe in its air for the first time since I was escorted out of the country to be adopted in the U.S. in August 1974 as an 8-month-old infant. I was not there to kiss the ground, nor to weep for joy or sorrow, nor even to claim any kind of birthright. I was prepared to see everything as it was and has remained.

Ho Chi Minh City (Sài Gòn) was decked out with bright red banners carrying canary yellow inscriptions on them and retro socialist billboards in anticipation of commemorating the 40th anniversary of the end of the Vietnam War (as Westerners call it) or the American War (as the Vietnamese call it), and the country's independence. My first impressions of the city and its people were that they were living as if nothing was out of reach and the future was theirs for the taking. For many of Vietnam's citizens April 30th has become an annual nationalist holiday, much like our Fourth of July. It is a day that signifies ritualized pomp and something vaguely historic, yet you're always glad to see it come because it mainly means a period of respite from the daily grind.

But, for me, phantom memories of the smoldering carnage of the war's end continues to singe my psyche and leave its mark. Each day I spent in Ho Chi Minh City I was aware that my subconscious was aware that I had once been, very briefly, a citizen of the Republic of Vietnam (i.e. South Vietnam). Whenever that realization came to my mind's surface, it was difficult to reconcile it with what was going on all around me. It was like I was one of those war relics at the museum that came to life. I was no longer lying dormant inside a dusty plexiglass case; my skin was absorbing the sun's rays, my stomach was enjoying the refreshing coolness of the local "333" beer, and people walked past me like any other tourist with a camera.

In my mid-20's I started researching the era in which I was born, paying particular attention to stories and images of children in South Vietnam. I regularly encountered the terms "dust of life," "war waif," and "Saigon street urchin" in books and magazine articles. These words would also appear in photo captions alongside full-page black-and-white portraits of infants, toddlers, and older children in various state of undress — their eyes unable to say what they have seen. I would stare at these children's faces and feel as if I were standing among them. Contrary to this feeling, my mind and body prevented me from believing that I shared any affinity with these kids, given the structures of the environment I was adopted into, and convinced me that my story was far removed from their timeless visages. Even so, the faces in those photos continued to speak in a language that rang true whenever my ears were attuned to their calls.

My status as an adopted person from Vietnam was little known outside of my immediate family and friends. I did my best early on in childhood to conceal and then force myself to forget my origins in Vietnam. Doing so allowed me to be just another "red-blooded American" kid growing up in a predominately white U.S. suburb.

Whenever I saw documentary footage of the War, I distanced myself from the images and shied away from any inner recognition of my immigrant/adoptee status that might separate me even more, emotionally and physically, from family and friends. My eyes refused to meet those on the screen or the page who were more related to me than I could ever acknowledge.

My budding adolescence eventually made me more conscious of my surroundings and more wise to the way people treated me based on my perceived difference, both in skin tone and immigrant status. Usually, I did not handle these situations with much grace but instead with spirited irreverence and thinly veiled hostility. As I struggled to keep up the appearance of being "the good son" to my adoptive parents, a special kind of anger took root inside me. It was fueled by the recognition that I was missing entire chapters in my life. Whole volumes containing innumerable pieces of information that could reconnect me to the circumstances and people behind my birth and adoption were unaccounted for. On especially dark days I'd catch sight of myself on the edge of a void, throwing question after question down into it, with no answers ever materializing. As my vision became sharper, the more cracks I noticed – cracks in school walls, cracks in friends' faces, cracks in mirrors, and cracks all over my body.

When I think about when, where, and how I came to be on this planet, the chaos and randomness of brutish violence, angelic redemption, and pure indifference blend together to create a conflagration from which I was delivered into the arms of strangers in a strange land. Someone watching out for me foresaw that any delay in my removal from the perilous situation unfolding in that humid and rugged Southeast Asian country could result in a five-fold increase in injury or fatality. It has been estimated that over 6 million tons of bombs (the equivalent of 640 Hiroshima-sized atomic bombs) were dropped on Vietnam, a country roughly the size of New Mexico. Such an atrocious amount of munitions aimed primarily at the rural, agrarian regions of the country left countless children orphaned and drove millions of people into urban centers that had barely enough resources for these internal refugees. When I contemplate the death toll among children in my age group at the time and the wasteland awaiting those who survived to live on in the desolation, pangs of survivor's guilt clench my insides. I don't feel blessed and I don't feel lucky; sometimes I just don't want to feel.

"Product of war." There's no denying that the war did make me an orphan and, subsequently, made me available for adoption. My flesh and bones were poured into the tumultuous cast of mortal combat, peeled out, and set aside to cool and harden into a tannish little body for consumption.

In the American public's imagination and memorialization of the "Fall of Saigon" or "Black April", and in our history books, war movies, documentaries, and public memorials the Vietnamese are virtually erased from Vietnam. If they are mentioned, they are generally portrayed as hapless peasants or notorious tunnel rats. I am instructed to believe that my exile from Vietnam was a fortuitous act of fate and it was up to well-meaning Westerners to shepherd me out of the country in order to give me a proper upbringing. With historical amnesia setting in, the decisions and actions which contributed to the demise of the country of my birth are catalogued and filed in archive rooms all over the country. Once collective memory fades, they are then further redacted and finally shredded.

As the 40th anniversary of the end of the Vietnam War approaches, I expect to be exposed to old-guard ideologies and unreconciled pain stemming from that period of our nation's history. It will be like I'm standing there as some kind of vessel charged with keeping old Vietnam vets' darkest secrets safe. Rattling sabers will want to re-write their legacies on my steel exterior in hopes of both shielding themselves from the residual heat of the war's aftermath and preventing me from prying too deeply into the layered myth of "Peace with Honor." In spite of their best intentions, I will be all too cognizant of that moment in history when I could have been just another crushed corpse for fleeing people to step over on their way to planes, helicopters, and boats to escape the surging People's Revolution. Suffice it to say, though, I have grown to appreciate and then ignore other people's historical interpretations of a war that not only took everything from me, but also gave me everything I know, which I unfortunately take for granted (every once in a while).

I am slowly coming to understand and accept that I am a son of Vietnam even though I do not speak its language and do not live within its borders. My re-emergence in the motherland at the beginning of April reinforced for me the legacy I inherited both in blood and in name. I found myself there as both a singular and an eternal presence, like a glint of light reflected off the wings of a dragonfly flitting over a crowded pond.

68

NO DREAM TOO LASTING

A Brief History of the Vietnamese in Germany

Like it was yesterday, I still remember when I ran across this Vietnamese guy in Berlin when I was walking up the steps from one of the main subway exits. In the fall of 1994, I was on holiday from university and it was one of my dreams to step foot in Berlin. The man had a look on his face as if he knew me and he proceeded to speak to me in Vietnamese, holding out a pack of cigarettes, like he wanted me to just take it. He wore a baseball cap perched on his head, as well as a wrinkled blazer and a pair of dark slacks. His face was reddish brown and quite chapped from exposure to the sun and the wind. This man was a little shorter than me, but he looked to be twice my age. I stared at him, hesitated, and finally just brushed him off and walked away. It wasn't because I didn't smoke, but rather due to the fact that I had more questions than small talk and a language barrier would allow.

By the time I left Berlin, I had seen several of these Vietnamese cigarette vendors standing near subway openings, trying to sell their tobacco wares. After doing some research many years after I had graduated from college, I figured out that I didn't just encounter some anonymous Vietnamese guy in Germany, but rather members of an illicit society who had unwittingly played a part in an elaborate story that few people have heard about.

Vietnamese people have settled into areas of the globe where few people would expect them. I think that's why I felt such a disconnect when I came into contact with that one guy on a busy sidewalk in

Berlin; my mind scrambled for a plausible reason as
to why a Vietnamese person would be in the capital
of Germany of all places. Not in the least did I find it
ironic that someone could have leveled the same
accusation at me: "What are {you} doing here?"

The beginning of the influx of Vietnamese
emigration to Germany can be tied to the end of the
war in April 1975. The government of the new
socialist republic of Vietnam found itself heavily in
debt to several other socialist countries, one of them
being East Germany. In order to alleviate some of that
debt, the Vietnamese government agreed to send
several thousand contract workers to East Germany
so they could supplement the East German workforce.
"At one time there were almost 100,000 Vietnamese
from northern Vietnam fuelling the GDR [German
Democratic Republic] economy and making up the
largest non-German ethnic group in the country."[1]
Vietnamese scholars and bureaucrats also traveled to
East Germany for cultural and economic exchanges
all in the name of cultivating "socialist brotherhood."

However, instead of the East German government
rolling out the welcome mat for this substantial
foreign workforce, it did its best to socially isolate
these workers and, when their contracts expired,
expeditiously saw them to the door. Permanent
residency was not an option for those Vietnamese
workers who wanted to stay in East Germany longer
than their contracts permitted and gaining East
German citizenship was also out of the question.
Regular interaction with the East German population
was a rarity, as the Vietnamese were placed in drab,
poor quality dormitories where their movements were
heavily restricted inside and out. Vietnamese women

were not allowed to get pregnant while they were under contract to work in East Germany, and if they did, then they either had to undergo an abortion or be sent back to Vietnam. If the Vietnamese violated any of these segregationist measures, they would be harassed, or jailed, by the police and more than likely deported. Not only did this kind of social control dampen any enthusiasm the Vietnamese laborers may have had for this little social(ist) experiment, but it also caused a wide rift to develop between the East Germans and their foreign workforce. This dissociation led to several high-profile anti-foreigner attacks in the early to mid-1990s after German reunification.

Suffice it to say, most of the Vietnamese who came to East Germany weren't exactly there out of some shared ideal of socialist solidarity either, but primarily for personal economic reasons. However, when the two Germanys reunited after forty years of separation in 1990, a substantial portion of the foreign workforce was laid off (14,000 people within the first four months of 1990[2]) with even more to come. Once a vital cog in the East German industrial machine, many Vietnamese found themselves in a virtual no man's land without a job and without any legal status in the reunified Germany. The German government eventually offered each Vietnamese guest worker $2,000 and a one-way plane ticket back to Vietnam. An estimated 50,000 Vietnamese took up the offer and left Germany. Those who chose to stay either applied for political asylum or risked residing in the country illegally. Less than 2% of those who applied were granted asylum.

Unemployment and continued social ostracization precipitated the Vietnamese entrance into the illicit cigarette trade in mainly eastern German cities. Polish tourists to East Germany are thought to have been the first group to start selling untaxed cigarettes out in public. While waiting for asylum to be granted or wishing to make some quick money, or for the simple fact that they didn't want to go back to Vietnam, a significant number of Vietnamese men risked their lives by becoming cigarette vendors. They soon took over the business from Polish and other Eastern European immigrants.

At lucrative spots it was estimated that up to 600 cartons of cigarettes could be sold in a single day for a profit of 2 to 4 Deutsche Marks each, while vendors in less attractive spots could still sell 10 to 20, and sometimes 100, cartons a day. That would mean the monthly earnings would be between several hundred to several thousand Deutsche Marks[3].

But, as with any black-market activity, the profitable end of the spectrum is balanced out by the horrendous toll it takes on those directly involved and anyone who comes in contact with them. In the mid 1990s, Vietnamese extortion gangs, whose membership was based on regional ties, clans or mutual associations back in the home country, grew in their influence and control over Vietnamese vendors and the illicit cigarette trade. It became impossible for cigarette vendors to work independently because they were forced to pay a benefactor for the right to sell cigarettes at a certain spot and for protection from rival gangs. In Berlin, murders among Vietnamese cigarette vendors and gang members increased every year from 1993 to

1996. In 1996 alone 15 homicides were recorded
within the Vietnamese community. These were
readily attributed to the illicit cigarette trade.
Horrendously, in May 1996, six Vietnamese, who
were known to the police as illicit cigarette vendors,
were executed in their apartment. "As investigators
found out later, the killers had tried to learn the
whereabouts of a gang leader to take revenge for the
murder of one of their own vendors three days
earlier[4]."

Luckily, the German police were largely
successful in breaking up two of the biggest
Vietnamese extortion gangs by arresting several of
their leaders. Later, in the summer of 1997, six more
gang members were apprehended. Today, not more
than 10 small bands of people are known to extort the
rest of the cigarette vendors and none have the
influence or power once held by the gangs in the early
1990s.

When East Germany's government and economy
were dissolved and incorporated into the greater
Federal Republic of Germany, many of its major
industries and services either folded or were bought
up by investors and entrepreneurs from western
Germany and elsewhere. Countless workers and
bureaucrats were let go and they soon found out that
their skill sets were either unwanted in the new
economy or wholly inadequate to fulfill the needs of a
more high paced and technologically savvy economy.
This mass unemployment, coupled with the shock of
the melding together of two different societies and
national histories after 40 years of separation, caused
much resentment and fear among the people in cities
and towns across the eastern territories. Added to this

economic/social instability were still thousands of foreign guest workers who were also scrambling for a living in this newly formed country. It didn't take long for the tension and resentment among the German citizenry to become palpable. In the early 1990s, right wing extremist political parties attempted to take advantage of the growing disaffection and disillusion felt by many Germans by actually making inroads in some local elections. However, it was the actions of neo-Nazi youths that garnered the most attention on the evening news around the world.

Video footage of skinhead mobs stomping in unison through narrow streets in numerous German cities, saluting the ghost of Hitler and carrying big red flags with a swastika in the middle, was broadcast all over the world. Vietnamese immigrants, along with other non-white immigrants, in Germany were caught in this maelstrom of xenophobia that seemed to have washed over the country. The event that most graphically illustrated the culmination of extremist violence toward foreigners in Germany occurred in the coastal city of Rostock on August 24, 1994. That night hundreds of people gathered around a housing complex where asylum seekers were staying and eventually the inhabitants had to be evacuated by the police because of the charged and anger-filled atmosphere. Unfortunately, near that complex was a building that housed about 150 Vietnamese guest workers. Without the aid of police, who, for some unexplained reason, momentarily pulled back from the vicinity of the building, the inhabitants could only watch on helplessly while skinheads attacked the building and threw Molotov cocktails into it, trapping the people inside. Nearly 100 of the building's residents were killed in that melee.

In order to facilitate the orderly departure of Vietnamese immigrants from Germany, the Vietnamese and German governments agreed to repatriate 40,000 Vietnamese immigrants in 1995 who were either denied asylum or were living illegally in Germany. By the year 2000, Vietnam was to have repatriated all 40,000 of them and Germany would have paid out $72 million US to assist with the process[5]. But, this plan of action soon fell apart when the Vietnamese government proceeded to put up barrier after barrier in front of these very immigrants by imposing certain conditions on their lawful return. For instance, the overseas Vietnamese in Germany had to demonstrate that they did not have dual citizenship, that they lived in Vietnam, and that they were being sponsored by economic or social organizations or individuals. The government of Vietnam also refused to repatriate those Vietnamese who did not accept Germany's original offer in 1990 of payment and a one-way plane ticket back to Vietnam. This left the majority of the 40,000 immigrants, who were due to be repatriated, in the lurch. It is no wonder so many Vietnamese immigrants who came to Germany as contract workers, guest workers or asylum seekers felt as though they lived in a no man's land: they neither felt completely comfortable in Germany, nor, apparently, did their home country of Vietnam want to have anything to do with them.

In spite of the hardships and uncertainty, many of the Vietnamese living in Germany have accepted their odd situation and have begun laying down roots in their adopted country. Because of relaxed immigration rules put into effect in 2003, the German government has allowed more and more immigrants to become permanent residents and is slowly altering the definition of what it legally means to be a German citizen. It is doing away with the centuries-old "blood law", wherein one could only be a German citizen if one could demonstrate exclusive German lineage in their family history.

In eastern Berlin, the Vietnamese have established and developed the Vietnam-Handelszentrum (Vietnamese business center). This is a place where their small businesses thrive, and where people can congregate and reconnect with something more culturally familiar. It can be assumed, as with any other immigrant population, that the children of Vietnamese who emigrated to Germany during the 1970s and 1980s have already assimilated to the dominant culture. They probably mix and match both Vietnamese and German culture according to their own individual whims and wills, dreams and ambitions. Year after year, and decade after decade, these two cultures will learn to live side by side, if not already intertwined.

The inevitability of cultural assimilation and grudging social acceptance of immigrants in Germany reminds me of a quote from a Vietnamese immigrant named Thanh, who was a contract worker in East Germany during the 1980s. Back then Thanh accepted the German government's offer of money to go back to Vietnam in 1990, but then due to a desire for a better standard of living for his family decided to leave Vietnam for Germany again. He said, "As time goes on, I know I cannot settle again in Vietnam. My children are now German, not Vietnamese[6]."

[1] Trapped in the twilight zone: A Vietnamese asylum seeker in Germany tells Kieran Cooke how he was once invited to work in Europe but is now unwanted by both the east and west, Kieran Cooke, FT, 09/22/01.

[2] Foreign "Contract Workers" of the Former GDR Unwanted in the United Germany, FECL 21, 12/93 / 01/94.

[3] The Nicotine Racket: Trafficking in Untaxed Cigarettes: A Case Study of Organized Crime in Germany, Dr. Klaus von Lampe.

[4] The Nicotine Racket: Trafficking in Untaxed Cigarettes: A Case Study of Organized Crime in Germany, Dr. Klaus von Lampe.

[5] Employment and Asylum in Germany, Immigration Laws, 07/95.

[6] Trapped in the twilight zone: A Vietnamese asylum seeker in Germany tells Kieran Cooke how he was once invited to work in Europe but is now unwanted by both the east and west, Kieran Cooke, FT, 09/22/01.

Archaeology of the Mind (or How I Have Henry Kissinger to Thank for My Existence)

I've long lived with the fear that my birth is evidence of a crime committed and forgotten. Some days I entertain the insane thought that, if it weren't for Henry Kissinger helping to prolong the Vietnam War, I wouldn't have been born. From across the Pacific Ocean, this German immigrant played matchmaker between my mother and my father in the early spring of 1973, inching them closer and closer, until I came sputtering out into the damp, warm air of a country that found itself on its last legs.

I was born in early December of 1973, possibly at the hospital in the Gia Dinh district of Saigon, to a Vietnamese mother and American father. But about five years prior to my birth, in 1968, Henry Kissinger traveled along as an adviser to the Lyndon Johnson administration when representatives from the United States and North Vietnam finally met in Paris to negotiate a peace settlement and bring an end to hostilities between the two nations for the first time since 1965.

Ken Burns' and Lynn Novick's most recent documentary "The Vietnam War" attends to the drama that unfolded at those negotiations. However, one would be remiss in not considering another documentary, called "The Trials of Henry Kissinger." This one was based on Christopher Hitchens' 2001 Harper's Magazine article, "The Case Against Henry Kissinger," which put forth the theory (now accepted as fact) that, behind Johnson's back, Kissinger was secretly passing on key information from the negotiations to Richard Nixon's campaign team.

The U.S. and North Vietnamese were reaching an agreement that could end, or at least halt, hostilities between the two countries. Nixon promised South Vietnam's President Nguyen Van Thieu that his future administration would continue to support Thieu's regime against an inevitable Communist takeover. On cue, the South Vietnamese contingent backed out of the peace negotiations, and the process fell apart.

Having promised the American people "peace with honor," Nixon won the presidency in November 1968, and he tapped Kissinger to be his new national security adviser. As a result of Kissinger's and Nixon's backroom dealing, the war throughout Southeast Asia actually expanded and went on for another seven years. I noticed the documentary by Burns and Novick failed to pinpoint Kissinger's pivotal role in Nixon's political maneuvering.

Kissinger's activities to favor Nixon's presidential campaign by deliberately scuttling a serious attempt to end a disastrous and out-of-control war were both cavalier and cruel.

As the war progressed, many Americans read about orphaned Vietnamese children in the newspaper and saw them on the evening news. They believed they had a moral responsibility to take care of those less fortunate and to open their hearts and homes to the children of a war that they forgot their country prosecuted and escalated.

Regardless, the implied politicized message was that Americans were more moral than those "godless Communists," aka the Vietnamese, and that only

Americans could provide an infinitely better outcome to these castaways. Under the protection of the U.S. military — and with the support of countless donations — several religious groups established Christian-based orphanages that inadvertently took the place of indigenous methods of child welfare. With so much of South Vietnam overwhelmed by the casualties of war, enterprising "good Samaritans" took up the mantles of healer and savior.

The longer U.S. military and civilian personnel stayed in the country, the more prostitution and intermarriage produced children of mixed race. These "Amerasians" were commonly orphaned or abandoned because of a mix of poverty, national (and personal) shame, and sheer neglect on both sides. The Western media portrayed these children as caged animals, unwanted by their unfeeling mothers and missing-in-action fathers. To soothe their conscience and fulfill a sense of obligation to those fathered by their countrymen, Americans advocated for the adoption of these Amerasians. Intentionally or not, the adoption of these children became the Trojan horse for institutionalizing the adoption of Vietnamese children across the board.

My own adoption by Americans was facilitated in the summer of 1974. With it came my parents' awkward and prolonged silence about the country in which I was born and the war that belched me forth. Ever since I can remember, the American foot soldier and, by extension, the people of the United States were cast as the victims of the Vietnam War. They represented the twin beacons of freedom, fighting for a noble cause. In the face of such rhetoric, I was expected to demonstrate compliant gratitude. This left me very early on open to disinformation and without a defense against emotional manipulation. No one wanted to acknowledge the unpleasant paradox of thousands of Vietnamese children living in the country whose citizenry readily accepted a war waged against the very people who conceived them.

Watching "The Vietnam War" documentary series forced me yet again to confront the truly mind-numbing thought: Henry Kissinger scheduled the deaths of thousands upon thousands of my countrymen (both Vietnamese and American) so that I may breathe at this very moment.

Grown in the USA

When the topic of Asian American history and identity is addressed in our media, academic circles and government policy, there is usually scant mention of people who were adopted from Asia. Awareness of this subgroup of Asian Americans has been gaining traction over the past two decades, but the discussion seems to still be limited to origin stories of Asian immigrants, past and present, and the process of their assimilation into the fabric of American society. It is quite evident now that people who were adopted from Asia and raised in predominantly White households skew and complicate the cultural and political markers of what it means to be of Asian descent living in America. Rather than relying on superficial appearances, people who involve themselves in Asian American issues and studies need to readjust their inclusion parameters to take into account those who look the part but who have been swimming in the mainstream for most of their lives.

Back in the early eighties, I interviewed four adults in their mid to late twenties, whom I personally knew, about the nature of their adoptions and how they viewed themselves within and without the Asian American community. All four people were placed with parents who are Caucasian (except for one, whose mother came from Korea) and grew up in predominately Caucasian communities.

Lim grew up in eastern Kentucky, Pat grew up in Auburn, Washington, Kendra grew up in Kent, Washington, and Robert was raised 20 miles outside of Boston. Because of their backgrounds as adoptees, finding similarities in their formative experiences was not unexpected. However, each individual exhibited independent viewpoints and chose paths in life that spoke to their unique outlooks. Robert deftly characterized the dilemma faced by many Asian American adoptees. "I think that one of the greatest strengths and weaknesses of being adopted is that we are not easily categorized."

In America, people grow up on ethnic labels and either accept or deny them based on their own interests and calculations to change or gain status within the social milieu they find themselves. In this country, ethnicity and race take on a life of their own, and people are regularly challenged to affiliate themselves with a group in order to earmark them for future considerations. Regardless, the four adoptees I interviewed expressed a remarkable ambivalence toward the category "Asian American." Lim, adopted from South Korea, explained "Obviously, I am Asian and I am American, so just by that definition, yeah, sure, I identify with the term. I can't say historically because I think for an adoptee your history starts with you." She also expressed the ability to "float" between identities when circumstances called for it. Robert, adopted from the former South Vietnam, broke down the definition of Asian American even further: "Nobody is defining what it means to be 'Asian.' Does it mean 'of Asian descent,' in a racial sense? Does it mean 'of Asian heritage,' in an ethnic sense? These terms are used interchangeably," which "in my personal opinion cheapens and devalues the immense diversity within our population." Kendra, another Vietnamese adoptee, recounted a disillusioning episode when she joined the Asian American student union at the college she attended. As a way to reconnect with her heritage and bond with other Asian Americans, she joined this specific student union, but "as soon as people would make conversation, I (would) get the comment that, 'You're white, you're too white.' I never really understood that. I felt it was another community that (was) turning me away." Pat, another Korean adoptee, explained the phenomenon of being neither here nor there, when he lamented, "I guess they're defined as 'Tweeners,' meaning that you don't belong to the Korean community, but you don't belong to the American community, so a lot of adoptees are in the middle."

Rapid assimilation and denial of racial asymmetries, and sometimes even language differences, were normal methods to acculturate and assimilate transracial adoptees from as early as the 1950s. The adopted children from Asian countries were affected by the naivety of colorblind altruism practiced by their well-meaning parents in many ways they couldn't have anticipated. Adoptive parents believed they were doing the right thing by glossing over the difference between their own skin color and their child's, thus hoping to sidestep the very real corrosive effects of racism.

These parents thought they were taking a leap of faith by embracing a biological anomaly and forcing society to realize the error of its ways and accept those orphaned children as its own. It was assumed that a force shield would protect the children by virtue of their living under the tutelage of Caucasian parents. Historical White privilege was so convinced that its adopted children would command the same respect and build the same self-esteem as their benefactors. "I was pretty much raised to be Caucasian with Caucasian values and beliefs - the belief that, 'Yeah, you can do anything. You're an American,'" said Lim. Pat held no punches when asked how he dealt with growing up in a predominately White community. "Somehow I kind of found my own way. I definitely don't feel a part of the Asian community at all. The reasons are mainly environment. I grew up in an all-Caucasian town, basically. So the environment definitely creates the people you know, and all my friends are white." Within the past 10 years, however, adult transracial adoptees of Asian descent have advocated and formed associations to carve out their own identity on their own terms. They have been motivated to not only interrogate and, in many cases distance themselves from, their mainstream Caucasian upbringing, but also disavow the pressure to identify with a specific nationality and/or culture simply based on their outside appearance. Many transracial adoptees have opted to create their own narratives about their coming-of-age experiences and even manipulate, and multiply, their identities according to their moods and purposes.

One of the most difficult, but common, things for many Asian American adoptees to do is attempt to reconnect with their birth country's people, history and culture. Everyone has had their own misadventures and successes navigating this venture, and it was no different for Lim, Kendra, Robert and Pat. Lim had made a conscious effort to understand the country from which she came. "If I go to a Korean store or go to some of the shops, I feel comfortable with that. I don't feel self-conscious. I do feel bad when I can't speak to them in Korean, but I don't feel like I can't go there or that they look at me different if I go there." She had a friend in Chicago who felt welcomed into the community from day one. However, she also had friends who never felt a part of that community and would always feel the 'adoptee' bulls-eye attached to their backs. In April 2001, Kendra and Robert went back to Vietnam with a group of adoptees to tour the country and received quite a shock when she was "laughed at by the government officials who looked at my passport and saw that I was really born in Vietnam. Maybe some hard feelings surrounding that. That feeling that I didn't look like anybody else was really hard."

Perhaps it would be easy for one to assume that adoptees set themselves up for some hurtful realities when interacting with their birth cultures. The level of cultural disconnect and language barriers do no one any favors when it comes to attempting to reintroduce yourself to a community that has learned to forget your brief existence in their care. That said, it isn't out of the realm of believability that adoptees would become curious about and desire to engage with people with whom they share physical traits. It is, of course, a natural inclination for people to want to belong and be accepted by others who look like them. As adults, many adoptees came away with the feeling that something in their lives was missing and they had to find whatever it was they were lacking. Whether they came to this decision with realistic goals in mind or simply overcompensated for their feelings of loss depended on the individual.

Claiming one's heritage or identifying with exclusively one group of people is not an easy enterprise. Such things as heritage, culture and language are beyond uniform codes. Exceptions to the rule can be found in every nationality and ethnic group. To say that there is only one Asian American community is too simplistic. On the other hand, to argue that the term 'Asian American' has no meaning, history or members with shared experiences would be wholly inaccurate. For many adoptees of Asian descent the stress of not knowing where one fits into the scheme of mainstream society can build exponentially over time. Robert boiled this point down to this statement: "Even if I don't fully understand my own Vietnamese heritage, I do understand and have lived the feeling of hate, racism and prejudice. Unfortunately, this is a universal experience that all Asian Americans have felt in one way, shape or form. Because of the tendency of others to categorize us into one group, I identify strongly with Asian Americans, because I am one."

Good Morning, Phan Duc To

Movies in modern times have always been the most effective propaganda tool to "educate" the populace about the significance of certain historical events that affect the nation-state, especially wars. These films demand that the audience side with the protagonist, the hero(s), and identify with their plight, their existential conflicts, and cheer on their methods to triumph over a dilemma and bring the story to a heroic and satisfactory conclusion. These grand, and meta, narratives have even taught us how to feel about the country we call "home" and how to view our fellow (non)citizens. This is no less true of Barry Levinson's "Good Morning, Vietnam," a historical dramedy, as I like to refer to it. The star, Robin Williams, is the protagonist who plays the naive doughboy thrown into the middle of a pack of wolves in a foreign country he could never truly feel at home in. The audience is expected to cheer when the hero survives various torments during his "combat" tour and when he reinforces America's unquestionable benevolence after he shouts into the air of a curiously de-populated slum, "We're here to help this country!"

According to Levinson's re-imagining of the war in "Good Morning, Vietnam," it seems that in 1965 everyone in the 'Nam, especially the grunts on the front lines, is in need of a resident funnyman to make them all forget about their woes and homesickness. That's where Robin Williams, playing shock jock Adrian Cronauer, comes in. This irreverent, fresh-mouthed airman is supposedly not your typical career GI, but as soon as his feet hit the tarmac, he is chasing tail with the best of them. ["May Day! May Day!

Dragon Lady with incredible figure at 11 o'clock.
Stop the car!…They're quick and fast and small. I
feel like a fox in a chicken coop."] Whoops!
(Ssshhh!) Sorry, that's top secret. [Circle red, cross
out.]

The only thing the audience is authorized to
believe is that Cronauer is just a likeable guy brought
in to do a little radio show in the middle of an
escalating war. But we can ill afford not to scrutinize
this G-man when he struts around thinking he can
have any Vietnamese woman walking down the
street. In fact, he sets his sights on Trinh, a young
woman going about her business in a spotless, white
ao dai, and follows her into an English language class
where he promptly schemes his way into the
instructor role just to hit on her. He wants her so bad
that he superficially befriends one of the students,
Tuan, who is conveniently Trinh's brother.

Throughout the movie, Cronauer is lavished with
sympathy and moral support because he's portrayed
as a resilient man pitted against a couple of no-
nonsense, humorless superiors. He becomes just one
of the guys, a good-natured marshmallow like all the
other young American soldiers out sun-tanning on the
patrol boats or playing a game of football in front of
ammunition crates. Cronauer speaks to them in a
language they all have in common, the language of
rock 'n' roll. But in order to get the audience fully on
his side, to help the viewers distinguish the good from
the bad, the black from the white, the helpers and the
helpless, a perfect, dark-faced foil is needed to place
Cronauer's good nature in stark relief. Enter Tuan,
aka Phan Duc To, aka the Wonder VC: today your
friend, tomorrow your enemy — "I no like you, sir.

You're phony, like American and French before you."

Turns out that Tuan is the real tragic hero in this movie. But no one would ever know it because he's given the role of garbage heap onto which the Americans can dump their insults, pettiness, ego trips and Teflon arrogance. He's infantilized, like all the other "Vietnamese" in the movie, as Cronauer illustrates by kidding, "If I don't get to my class, there's going to be a lot of Vietnamese speaking in short, choppy sentences." Therein lies the seething prejudice of the American authority figures charged with saving this land from itself. Since the natives can't speak the language of power, they are prohibited from speaking to the audience at all, thus stripped of any shared humanity. Cronauer continuously condemns his students to toddlerhood because of their "short, choppy sentences" and childlike incoherence when they try to communicate with him. On top of all that, he subjects them to his barely masked contempt on the street, in local establishments and on the air, something that goes, unsurprisingly, over the locals' heads. Irony is finally swept from the script when, toward the end of the movie, Cronauer arranges for the students in his class to forgo their own language and customs and to adopt, instantaneously, the American Way, by playing baseball with juicy melons headed for market. Cronauer and his compatriots get to crack up and point at the cluelessness exhibited by the Vietnamese because of their complete lack of acumen and knowledge of the great American past time.

If that's not enough humiliation captured on celluloid, what's with the Cronauer character using

the nickname "Sparky" in place of Tuan's
Vietnamese name? Is "Tuan" too hard for the human
tongue to pronounce? Or is Cronauer simply above
proper modes of address? What a nickname, by gosh.
Kind of like "Corky" or "Gomer." Let's see, he uses
Tuan to try to get his sister into bed, he makes fun of
"fish balls" in his soup, once he tells Tuan he speaks
like "Tonto" and to spark further outrage he reserves
the exclusive right to call his "friend" a name unfit for
a stuffed toy. Sounds like a fair trade-off to me.

The most disturbing part of the film (apart from
Staff Sergeant Marty Dreiwitz, played by Robert
Wuhl, yelling at a Vietnamese MP, "Look, jerk off,
we're here fighting for your country!") is the fight
scene in the GI bar. All three grotesque Asian
stereotypes converge at this Orientalesque hang-out
for American military personnel. You have Jimmy
Wah, the "Oriental leprechaun" who's "light in the
loafers," the Vietnamese bar girls wearing skin-tight
mini-skirts flirting for beaucoup bucks and the VC
man-child disguised as Cronauer's guide and friend.
"Who brought the fucking gook? I said…" Tuan is
invited to sit with the privileged few, the ones who
are running his country into the ground.

Jimmy Wah's bar represents a small piece of
American Shangri-La, respite from the reality going
on just outside its doors. Tuan personifies the
emasculated "little Vietnamese kid," a brown-skinned
foreigner who finds himself at a table full of run-of-
the-mill American DJ nerds. Cronauer eventually
calls over to the prostitutes, Tuan's fellow citizens, or
"gals" as Private Garlick (played by Forest Whitaker)
likes to call them, with a fist full of đồng held out as
bait. Tuan watches with a bemused expression on his

face as the silk-clothed women slink on over and ease themselves on the men's' laps, and the men waste no time in consummating their flesh-and-blood fantasies — "How come I don't get one?" — hoping for more than just getting their egos stroked. As expected, the two jilted, thick-necked Übermenschen whose toys were taken away from them come ambling up to the table and unleash a torrent of racist barbs. Tuan, without a word (quiet on the set!), is ruthlessly pushed to the floor and, assuming his role as the White-Man's-Burden hero, Cronauer wields his witty sarcasm to poke fun at the soldiers' bigotry. For an encore, his sweaty forehead butts into the nose of one of the soldiers. [Cue beer bottles smashing to the floor. *Cut!* Mission accomplished.]

The fantasy all comes crashing down, though, when Adrian Cronauer finds out that all this time his "friend" Tuan was really his, and by extension America's, nemesis, Phan Duc To, a Viet Cong cadre. Cronauer's pained expression of betrayal takes center stage as he fixes his regal imperial gaze on surly, gaunt and alien male faces and bodies in search of the Judas hiding among them. Meanwhile, Tuan remains elusive, his voice suddenly surfacing and surrounding the disoriented Cronauer when he shouts brash retorts to the American's dismayed jabbering. "I fought to get you into that bar. And then you go and blow the fuckin' place up! I gave you my friendship and trust. Now they tell me that my best friend is the goddamn enemy!" This is too much for Tuan and he suddenly appears in a doorway and delivers an impassioned monologue in which he credibly shreds the Americans' goodwill gesture, blames them for indiscriminately killing his relatives and neighbors

("We're not human to them.") and throws it in Cronauer's sweaty, pained face.

In spite of Tuan getting to the truth of the matter, the audience needs to be reminded that this movie is Robin William's star vehicle, so Tuan's words once again fall on the radio personality's deaf ears ("Wait a minute. We're here to help this country!"). As soon as his tear-bloated face appears from behind an anonymous wall, Tuan is taken out of the equation because, jeez, what a killjoy, you know? Mr. Levinson doesn't want a pang of conscience, like Tuan, to become an impediment to Operation Rolling Chuckle, so thanks for the face time, little man, but take your complimentary gift bag and exit stage right.

As easy as it may be to downplay a character's impact, it is near impossible to quell the rising tide of history and deny the cyclical swelling of submerged memories. When it's obvious that Cronauer no longer wants to listen to how Tuan's life has changed since the Americans started digging in their heels and his reasons for why he is opposed to American involvement in his country's affairs, then that sounds the death knell for Tuan's/Vietnam's experiment in self-determination.

Suffice it to say, Adrian Cronauer comes off as a selfish, self-made man ("This will not look good on a resume!") who makes the classic American mistake of needing to feel and appear successful and vindicated, despite after-action reports to the contrary.

Operation Amerasian Redemption

Television wasn't my main form of entertainment growing up in the suburbs; reading books, magazines and the newspaper was. When I did watch TV, the programs I tended to gravitate to were action adventure tales of heroism and bravery. The car chases and firing of machine guns were the main attractions for me. Maybe because it was the way the shows were made or the way my mind was developing back in those days, but I don't remember ever really paying attention to the plot, character development or even the dialog of those serial productions. Any critical assessment of their social or political messaging and impact on the viewership's role in society was beyond me. Now, when I take a look back at them with many more years of life experience under my belt, I understand better the political culture I was brought up in and its overt and covert methods of enjoining me to an American exceptionalism. What had escaped my notice as a child comes to the fore now as a skeptical adult. It is that the heroes of the TV shows I glued myself to were all White and their foes were usually of foreign origin with thick accents and menacing darker skin.

Hunter, *MacGyver* and *Airwolf* were three network TV shows I rarely failed to miss back in the late '80s and early '90s. They took my imagination out of bleach-blonde suburbia and helped my mind go to places I only read in almanacs and saw in National Geographic magazines. The lead characters' derring-do and dashing bravery secured in my mind what a "real American" looks like and behaves in a world full of bad actors, so to speak.

What never occurred to me was that each of these shows had episodes in which an Asian-looking actor played an Amerasian child. Someone who resembled me actually played a role in one of the television programs I used to watch with such fandom, but which completely escaped my powers of observation. I saw myself but didn't recognize myself because to acknowledge that Asian character would irreparably disrupt and place my whole "adopted" world in disarray. It would have shattered me.

Technically, according to the U.S. State Department, I am one of thousands who was "born in Vietnam between January 1, 1962, and before January 1, 1976, fathered by an American citizen." Even more so now, the timing of these episodes that introduced Amerasian characters makes sense to me considering that the Amerasian Homecoming Act of 1988 was coming into its own and the 15th anniversary of the end of hostilities between Vietnam and the U.S. was about to be highlighted and reckoned with. Between 1989 and 1993, the Act allowed hundreds of Amerasians, along with their relatives and dependents, to emigrate to the United States. It was a practical, political and symbolic gesture by the U.S. government to make amends for the condition it left that relatively tiny country in after the war. However, books like *Surviving Twice: Amerasian Children of the Vietnam War* (by Trin Yarborough) and *The Dust of Life: America's Children Abandoned in Vietnam* (by Robert S. McKelvey) will duly inform you that the Amerasian Homecoming Act was hastily thought out, poorly funded and chaotically managed. Not only that, but, heart-wrenchingly enough, a lot of Vietnamese

Amerasians arrived in the country avidly believing
that they would be reunited with their fathers to live
life happily ever after in relative opulence. Suffice it
to say, fantasy and reality do not commonly mix, and
heartache was met with even more heartache when
these recent immigrants settled in to find themselves
in isolated, small-town environs that didn't
necessarily welcome them with open arms.

   With that as background to my recent observations
of Amerasian characters in TV programs I used to
revere, I found it quite amusing to watch a clip from
the show *Hunter* on YouTube where he confesses to a
young Amerasian guy that he, is his biological father:
"*Hunter* thinks an Amerasian boy may be his son and
believes the boy when he claims to be an innocent
bystander during a car theft that results in a murder."
(Episode #115, Season 6, air date 11/25/89). An
Amerasian character appears in two separate episodes
of *MacGyver*: "Second Chance," Episode #088,
Season 5, air date 10/16/89 ("MacGyver heads a
project bringing young Amerasians to the U.S. for
medical treatment. His companion finds a son he
didn't know he had."); and, "*The Coltons*," Episode
#130, Season 7, air date 10/14/91 ("The Colton
family aids an Amerasian girl fleeing from the
Chinese Mafia. She's the lone witness to a Chinatown
murder."). It seems there's a common thread running
through these shows where Amerasians accidentally
witness murders, thus placing one more heinous
burden on their troubled lives. Lastly, the show
Airwolf got in on the Amerasian action in the episode
"Daddy's Gone Hunt'n" ("A pilot James Whitmore
Jr. intends to steal a high-tech aircraft to ransom his
Amerasian son from the Soviets.").

It should be no surprise that I would have no recollection of these specific episodes featuring Amerasian characters. All that was on my mind when sitting in front of the TV was wanting to watch explosions and adrenaline-rushing action sequences. The fact that there were characters who represented my own ethnic and racial heritage and were stand-ins for a past relationship between two countries that bred my physical presence, in one way or the other, was completely not something I wanted to deal with, given that I was the only adopted mixed-race Vietnamese boy living in a small town in western New York.

Back then what popular culture taught me, and reminded me on a constant basis, was that the Caucasian faces on TV were generally the heroes, the ones with all the answers, and the Asian faces were the coolies, the gooks and the villains, the ones who got unceremoniously mowed down in droves. Childhood handed me the task of either taking or avoiding flak from random kids at school who saw me as not quite right (White). Ironically, my oppositional nature toward my classmates resulted from the very representations of Asians in the shows each of us watched and took our cues from. It only took 30 odd years for me to realize that pop culture had been reflecting racist attitudes already built into the well-oiled machine called America for close to two centuries. However, when it was time for primetime, my young self-esteem would be damned if it was going to be the only one left holding the rice hat.

Got war?

Due to numerous political and economic circumstances, as well as the sheer distance and passage of time, my body and consciousness were shielded from the ripping and tearing, the decay and degradation, and the dying moans of the American/Vietnam War: the one I had been born into, the one I wasn't told about it. Because the nation's disowned past hadn't been acknowledged, I had no way of recognizing my miniscule part in it. The suburbs in which I was raised, and the mentality that came with it, submerged the ir-reality of my past down to even more subterranean depths. My ability to 'pass' was accepted as a natural stage of development because not to do so would have been the death of me. In due time, though, the more my coagulated consciousness was stirred, the more detritus came floating to the top. The truths of war and the aftermath of decisions made in times of crises began overflowing makeshift boundaries and flooding the fertile fields of recall. Inconsistencies and uncomfortable silences broke through the placid surface of innocence.

Like many a rebellious teenager, I turned to music as a means of self-expression in order to go against the grain of inauthenticity I noticed all around me. Certain songs from specific bands helped me comprehend and interpret the state of the world. One of those bands was Metallica. Back in 1989, their song "One" alighted in me an awareness of the stultifying stillness and slack acceptance in my clouded surroundings.

"One" starts with a fade-in of strafing machine gun fire, exploding bombs and hovering helicopter blades. The clanging guitar notes mark the beginning of the descent into the main subject's personal torment. Blind, deaf and mute, with no limbs to speak of, the stump of a war veteran is kept alive through the indifferent orders of the military and the prurient nationalism of bureaucrats.

now that the war is through with me
I'm waking up, I cannot see
that there's not much left of me
nothing is real but pain now

No one pays attention to this man's humanity because he cannot speak for himself. His vulnerable physical state causes his caretakers to disregard his mental well-being ("I'm just a piece of meat that keeps on living."). All that this living war trophy can do is flip through his thoughts, dreams, nightmares and desires in his head, wasting time caught in a loop of childhood memories, and frantically sending out Morse code messages for help to end his misery ("Inside me I'm screaming, but nobody pays any attention. If I had arms, I'd kill myself; if I had legs, I could run away; if I had a voice, I could talk and be some kind of company to myself."). The parenthetical quotes come from movie clips from "Johnny Got His Gun" (1971), which were incorporated into the music video for "One".

At the time, I took the anti-war commentary literally and viewed the song and video as a common critique of the popular glorification of war in our society. With the benefit of hindsight, however, the

song was speaking to me on a much more innate
level. The speechless and devalued head and torso
lying on the hospital bed matched how I felt
whenever I thought about my actual role in my family
and community. I felt I was simply kept alive for
someone else's amusement, out of someone else's
sense of duty and responsibility or because I fit nicely
on the mantel for my parents' friends to gaze at and
comment upon.

fed through the tube that sticks in me
just like a wartime novelty
tied to machines that make me be
cut this life off from me

Manufactured to be an orphan in the war on the
Vietnamese, American society took pity on my
predicament once I was placed on its proverbial front
stoop. The predicament, though, is really this: how
does one bring in and raise a child of the enemy?
What sort of mental calculations had to be made to
reverse the fact that the people bringing me into their
community and making me a fellow citizen are the
very same ones who aided their government's willful
killing off of my countrymen and women? I can only
offer an educated guess on such a reversal of
fortunes: They gave me a second chance. And I could
take it or leave it.

My survival, my well-being and my peace of mind
were placed squarely on my shoulders. It was only
then that my new family, my community and the
people of the United States could reach over and pat
each other on the back and incredulously crow that at
least one good thing came out of the war: I am alive

because of their charity. Now, all that was left for me to do was to forgive and forget.

McCain & The Gook

John McCain the war hero. John McCain the brave American fighter pilot who endured five years in a cell in the "Hanoi Hilton" and was finally released in 1973. John McCain, who as a candidate vying for the presidency in 2000, once referred to his Vietnamese captors as "gooks". Not "those sons-of-bitches" or "those asshole guards", mind you, but simply "gooks". This irrevocable bigoted remark has been stuck in my craw since not only McCain's 2000 election bid, but also his election run in 2008.

It takes a lot of effort for a mealy-mouthed, over-privileged white man to act contrite and offer an apology for his utterance of a racist insult. When I analyzed McCain's apology back in 2000 it appeared to be a classic non-apology. This is when the offender instinctively minimizes the fallout precipitated by his thoughtless shitting-on of a whole people by reasoning that if he did offend anyone, then it's up to everyone, and not just him, to be big about it, forgive and forget, and finally move on. McCain responded admirably, and predictably, when someone in his election camp scribbled an apology on a notecard for him to crap out in front of the public so it could get a good, hard whiff of his contriteness. I found the following McCain quote on a website called "Quest for the Presidency", posted on March 1, 2000:

"There's no reason to. They understand. Many of them were in re-education camps and they were also tortured by some of these people," he said. "Look, I have very many good friends who are Vietnamese." He has said he would not use the word again. "I apologize if I offended anyone," McCain said recently. "But the validity of my statement, as I said, it was applied to a small group of sadists and murderers and the kindest word I could use about them was that. The rest of them (words) are not fit for family reading."

Let's break down this faux mea culpa:

"There's no reason to. They understand. Many of them were in re-education camps and they were also tortured by some of these people," he said.

The context behind this response was that someone asked McCain if he'd be willing to tackle the topic of his racist remark yet again when he visited Westminster, California, home to the largest Vietnamese expat community outside of Vietnam. Anyone who's familiar with this community knows that ultraconservative and anticommunist ideologies run deep and strong (much like the Cuban-American community in South Florida). Understandably, McCain felt he would have allies in his quest to free his neck from the racist yoke in which he placed himself and that those who had similar experiences in other tropical communist gulags would be supportive of his right to throw out the epithet "gooks" whenever he damn well pleased. Tragically, that was not far off the mark. If you were to read further down in the article found in "Quest for the Presidency", you would read of a divided public, mostly generational, whose hatred of old decrepit communists surpasses only their own self-hatred in a country that grudgingly allows them their Little Saigons, just as long as they don't seriously compete for jobs and public office.

"Look, I have very many good friends who are Vietnamese."

Typical. Every bigot caught with his pants down around his ankles with "nigger/gook/kike/spic, etc." written large on his forehead vociferously claims that he knows people or has friends who are from the very same race/ethnicity he just insulted. This is the classic method of temporarily using minority connections as a cudgel in order to fend off criticism of any lapses in judgment that the perpetrator swears will not occur again. Playing devil's advocate, what if such a person really does have close friends/acquaintances from the aggrieved party. Is this person implying that he was given the okay by them to use a specific epithet in their presence without recrimination, even though it disparages their very existence? Was McCain really given permission to throw out the word "gook" whenever it suited him at that moment? Was he actually leading us to believe that Vietnamese-Americans consented to this insensitive and disrespectful behavior because, well, hey, anything for a friend, right?

"I apologize if I offended anyone," McCain said recently.

If he offended anyone! I guess to McCain that's a big "If". He didn't offer any kind of genuine apology, folks. He was more committed to portraying the illusion of regret and with saving face before his WASPy friends. A real apology begins like so: "I apologize for doing (this and that). And, I promise I won't do it again." Also, it would make a significant difference if the offended party knew that the offender really learned something from his mistake. Of course, John McCain felt he was too much of a big shot to commit to a real apology, so he ended his mea culpa with this I-take-it-all-back-but-I'm-always-right-anyway statement:

"But the validity of my statement, as I said, it was applied to a small group of sadists and murderers and the kindest word I could use about them was that."

McCain insisted that he was using the word "gook" to refer only to a specific group of men who caused him and the other POWs at Hanoi Hilton harm and, for some of them, their untimely demise. Sorry, but this pitiful excuse has "willful ignorance" written all over it. The word "gook", or even "cracker", has never, and will never have, a laser guided system attached to it, aimed at a particular target and whose payload will only affect those persons who were selected for extinction.

"Gook" is a scattershot behemoth of an insult that puts everyone within the Asian community in the crosshairs of indiscriminate hostility. Throughout our country's prolific military history, "gook" has been utilized to condemn a whole swath of humanity who traces its ethnic roots to the continent of Asia. It is a word that helps dehumanize and rationalize any kind of mistreatment perpetrated on individuals within that targeted group.

In the summer of 2000, McCain made a campaign stop in Rochester, NY, my hometown. I was kidding around with a friend of mine and plotting on ways we could disrupt the political gathering and embarrass McCain for his lapse in judgment. I came up with the idea of making my own placard and writing in huge colorful letters, "Gooks for McCain!" I would've gone to the rally, held my sign aloft and screamed at the top of my lungs: "GOOKS FOR MCCAIN!! GOOKS FOR MCCAIN!!" Alas, I didn't have the balls to carry out that mission.

I'm such a gook.

Oops, I apologize. That won't happen again.

105

QUALMS

Li'l Sis

After multiple attempts at becoming pregnant, my
parents decided to adopt, first me and then my middle
sister, from South Vietnam. But, surprise, surprise,
not even two years after our adoption my youngest
sister Kerri is born. I don't have any recollection of
me holding her all bundled up in a white blanket on
my lap, as the photo taken at that time shows me
doing.

My parents ingrained in me the expectation that I
must take the lead in looking over my sisters when we
were out playing or at school, especially my youngest
sister. Being the eldest and a boy, I took both the
implied and explicit suggestion to be responsible for
my sisters as a physical challenge to the exclusion of
any deep empathy or compassion for them. When I
wanted my sisters to do something or my parents
asked me to tell them to do something, I wasn't
usually gentle about it; I either cajoled or threatened
them. This is the kind of training I received from my
parents, and I think that's how they pretty much
handled me too.

My behavior toward Kerri pretty much laid the
ground work for our divergent paths. I was too into
myself to realize the distance I was placing in
between us with my long silences and my sudden
outbursts. In many respects, Kerri felt just as lost
under my parents' roof as I did, but she expressed her
frustrations in a very different way.

If Kerri wasn't given her freedom, she took almost
every risk to just grab it and run with it. I admire her
so much now for having the guts to do that. But, I
also remember her crying behind her locked bedroom

door whenever she was grounded or shouting at my parents for being "unfair" because her brother "gets to do whatever he wants."

That's not to say that I didn't have my own escape routes in place. I made use of them by going inside myself, shutting myself down and shutting myself in my bedroom. As a developing young adult, I talked very little because I felt like I couldn't relate to anyone. In my household, it seemed like the only time my parents ever wanted to pay attention to me was when they expected me to go out and mow the lawn in the summer or shovel the driveway after a heavy snowfall, or particularly whenever they noticed my grades slipping. The only hobbies I enjoyed doing was drawing, riding my bike, reading and listening to music: all activities that don't necessarily require another person to be present. Passivity worked for me; all I wanted was for people to leave me alone and let me do whatever came to mind. My parents could never understand that. They avidly hosted parties, walked around the neighborhood to converse with neighbors and went out to dinner in large groups. They wanted me to be more like them; they chastised me whenever they found me in my room being quiet and reading, as if I were planning some kind of mutiny on the Good Ship Lollipop. I was tired of being scared of the outside world, of feeling there was no one I could connect with and especially angry for being taught that over-cautiousness and suppression of honest emotions were what added up to a life worth living.

My interactions with my sister Kerri, if not already meager, were severely limited as we both headed off to college or kept to our separate work schedules during summer and winter breaks. We worked those part-time jobs to replenish our beer and pizza money for the next semester, so we barely saw each other around the house. Post-college, we eventually moved out of our parents' house and into our own apartments on different sides of town. Finally, we found ourselves planning to move out of New York state at about the same time in the autumn of 2000 — she to Los Angeles to move in with her boyfriend and I to Seattle in order to satisfy my lust to go beyond what I already knew.

A few weeks before we were to leave Rochester, and knowing that I wouldn't see Kerri for a long time, I was inspired to write a poem for her called "hope your eye feels better." I was invited to be a featured poet at a reading held at the city's art museum, and I decided to unveil it there before my whole family. After I finished reading it, I looked up from the paper in my hands and saw that Kerri had tears in her eyes. It felt so good giving her a hug when I made my way back to my seat. There was so much I wanted to tell her, feeling so apologetic and bursting with guilt. But I did what I had always done and played the role of big brother and remained silent.

Salvage This

A few years before my father's passing he would increasingly tell me over the phone that he "loves me" as well as other curiosities, such as he's "proud of me" and that all he ever wanted was for me "to be happy."

You see, for me and my father, it was very much a case of too little too late because while in my father's charge, I didn't grow up with any clear assurance that he wanted to be my father at all. In his dealings with me, especially when we were alone together, it was difficult for him to mask the pretense between us.

Through the bifocals of adoption and transraciality/-ethnicity, I've had to re-evaluate my relationship with him as I remember it and experienced it. One thing really stood out in the process: although both of us had changed over the years, a couple key attitudes never did change. As far as choosing and planning to adopt me goes, I think my father saw himself as a Mr. Fix-It who possibly viewed the Vietnam War as an unfortunate misunderstanding between two nations that got a bit out of hand. He probably thought that if he could offer a safe haven to a child caught in the crosshairs, then he had just the kind of home any social worker would find acceptable. My father's generosity and volunteerism was well known in the community. It seemed that he always made time for his friends and immediate family members whenever they asked for his help, and even when they didn't. My father was quick to offer advice, especially on practical matters, and I have to admit he was usually on the mark. More than once I saw him as a tool. I don't mean that in the pejorative, insulting way, but instead in a metaphorical and sometimes literal sense. My father was a master electrician and overall handyman who possessed mathematical skills that he used to help countless people fix their house or get them out of run-of-the-mill engineering jams.

The confounding thing about my history and identity as an orphan, forced evacuee from Vietnam and fully assimilated American is that for all of my father's sympathy and generosity toward me, the unbridgeable distance between our hearts and minds would always be present.

My father had a tendency to take other people's word over mine. I'm sure in his own mind he thought he was only teaching me how to be evenhanded and fair in whatever situation I found myself in, but the unintended consequence was that I usually felt like that boy who cried wolf. No matter how vociferously I would explain myself or describe exactly what was happening to me, he would turn it around and ask what I had done to incur an insult or what I did to another kid who started a fight with me. My father made me feel that I had a difficult time being straight with him and that I had a tendency to lie in order to get my way. And, so, following in his expectations, I began telling insignificant and not so insignificant lies to him because I knew he wouldn't take me seriously.

Later on, as a teenager and as a young adult, I virtually told my father nothing about my life. Not only did we have completely different interests and misaligned personalities, but we allowed the silence between us to engulf us and erode any semblance of familial unity I may have shared with him. My father made it perfectly clear to me several times that he had invested a lot of time and money into my well-being and that as long as I was living under his roof, I was to bend to his commands and follow the rules he laid down in the house. In those days, the only "quality" time my father and I spent together was when he showed me how to do some menial task in the yard or when we sat in the same room to watch football, swimming in the awkward silence, until my mother came into the room to set down snacks for us.

The distance between my father and me was especially noticeable when it came to social situations both outside and inside the family. I saw that he had no problem introducing me to his friends or coworkers as his son, but once the niceties were over he would either usually ignore me or once in a while fashion some jokey jab at me for the exclusive benefit of those in the crowd. Granted, this type of behavior was typical of my father whenever we were out and about, and he rarely spared anyone within earshot. But he possessed no forethought or even afterthought with respect to how his own son reacted or responded to these little assaults on his evolving personhood. My father obviously didn't notice me not laughing or how I slowly turned inward and kept silent when these interactions were inevitable. I was subconsciously taking one more big step away from my father and he was unconsciously revealing to the world how artificial our bond was as father and son.

There was one year when I and my ex-wife were invited to come visit my father and mother at their rented condominium in a small town in Southern California. Newly retired, my parents would spend their winters in California, Arizona or Florida and invite relatives or friends to join them. I remember one of the pretenses of the visit was to watch that year's Super Bowl together. In the run-up to our visit, my mother hyped it up to me as an easy-going and fun getaway to reconnect with family members whom we haven't seen in a while and romp around on the nearby beach.

Perhaps the tap water in the condo was spiked with downer powder, but when both of us arrived everyone seemed to be on edge. It soon became apparent that my father and I were barely going to be speaking to each other. As was customary, I asked him a couple easy questions to get the ball rolling and he just answered them in a matter-of-fact, indifferent way. Perhaps it was jetlag, paranoia or total resignation on my part, but for the whole time I stayed there the look on my father's face conveyed to me that, if it were up to him, I wouldn't have been invited. Rarely did we cross paths while we took short trips outside of the condo and during those times when we found ourselves in the same room, we avoided eye contact. Meaningful conversations between us remained nonexistent. I really didn't know what was going on, but once again, I played the dutiful son and stayed out of my father's way. And then it happened: the proverbial straw breaking the camel's back.

I remember trying to get in on a conversation between my sister and her late husband and my cousin, but they blithely walked away from me with no acknowledgement of my eagerness to participate in the discussion. There I stood by the dining table, suddenly alone, and I jokingly lamented that no one in the family respected me. My father quickly looked up at me from the easy chair in which he was lounging in the living room and gave me one of his sardonic grins and remarked, "Yeah, you're right. No one respects you." There was no one else in the room to overhear his response to my lackluster complaint.

If my father meant what he said to me that day to be a joke, then I must admit it he did a fantastic job of disguising his true feelings. It had its usual effect of silencing me. I assessed it as just one more put-down to throw in with the others contained in my foot locker buried in the back of my closet.

Whenever the question of my father's role in my life comes to the fore, those old reliable feelings of gratitude, guilt and shame never fail to re-emerge. Even after his death about six years ago, I must confess that I'm still filled with charged, but inhibited, feelings. A Grand Inquisitor's voice booms down over me from up above: "Where would you be without him?" "Wasn't he the one who sacrificed everything in order for you to have a better life and this is how you repay him?" These aren't probative questions, I realize. Instead, they represent my conscience raking me over the coals in order to dislodge truths that I've denied myself from expressing due to an ingrained fear of losing any kind of love my father may have had for me. However, I've learned all too well that I do myself a disservice when I close my mouth and just smile. That's when I allow other people to assume that everything has been resolved and they can now change the subject.

In spite of our strange beginnings and semi-estranged plateau on which we held our ground, my father and I continued to shoot the breeze once in a while over the phone and had gotten quite good at it. I remember that whenever it came time to hang up the phone, my father never failed to tell me that he loved me. It sounded odd, at first, a bit too contrived. Eventually, I stopped doubting my father's intentions behind this sudden affection for me and I met his sendoff with the canned response of "Yep, love you too."

I couldn't think of anything better to say.

www.ingramcontent.com/pod-product-compliance
Lightning Source LLC
Chambersburg PA
CBHW032355280326
41935CB00008B/576